MODERN THEOLOGY
4. Reinhold Niebuhr

MODERN THEOLOGY

Selections from twentieth-century theologians
edited with an introduction and notes by

E. J. TINSLEY

4

Reinhold Niebuhr

1892–1971

LONDON
EPWORTH PRESS

ACKNOWLEDGEMENTS

The author and publisher are grateful for permission to quote in this series from the following works:

Church Dogmatics, Vol. I, 2; IV, 2, T. and T. Clark
Deliverance to the Captives, by Karl Barth, SCM Press
Kerygma and Myth, Vol. I; II, edited by H. W. Bartsch, SPCK
Christology, by Dietrich Bonhoeffer, Collins Publishers
Ethics, by Dietrich Bonhoeffer, SCM Press
Letters and Papers from Prison, by Dietrich Bonhoeffer, SCM Press
Sanctorum Communio, by Dietrich Bonhoeffer, Collins Publishers
The Cost of Discipleship, by Dietrich Bonhoeffer, SCM Press
Form Criticism, by Bultmann and Kundsin, Harper and Row, New York
Theology of the New Testament, Vol. II, by Rudolf Bultmann, translated by F. Grobel, SCM Press
Word and Faith, by G. Ebeling, translated by J. W. Leitch, SCM Press
The Nature of Faith, by Gerhard Ebeling, Collins Publishers
Selections from Karl Barth's Church Dogmatics, by H. Gollwitzer, T. and T. Clark
The Systematic Theology of Paul Tillich, by A. J. McKelway, Lutterworth Press
Beyond Tragedy, by Reinhold Niebuhr, James Nisbet and Co. Ltd
Leaves from the Notebook of a Tamed Cynic, by Reinhold Niebuhr, Harper and Row, New York
The Nature and Destiny of Man, Vol. I; II, by Reinhold Niebuhr, James Nisbet and Co. Ltd
World Come of Age, edited by R. Gregor Smith, Collins Publishers
The Death of God, by Gabriel Vahanian, George Braziller, Inc., New York

CONTENTS

PREFACE TO THE SERIES

The theologians represented in this series of five volumes of selections are those who, one can confidently say, are already assured of an important place in the history of twentieth-century theology.

In the case of each theologian I have tried to give a fair representation of the author's work although, inevitably, there are important aspects of his thought which I have not always found it possible to illustrate. I have throughout preferred to give substantial selections rather than short extracts because the qualities of the writing of the theologians in this collection require this treatment for proper understanding and illustration. Even so selections are no substitute for the original, and it is my hope that readers will become sufficiently interested in what is given in this series to want to go to the full range of the authors' complete works.

As well as being representative of an influential group of theologians I hope that the selections provided will be found to provide something of an integrated discussion among the writers themselves. I have, therefore, in making the selections included some which give an idea how these theologians view each other. The reader is given some indication of the views, say, of Barth on Bultmann or Niebuhr on Barth, and there are cross-references in the introduction and notes so that he can have an idea of what subjects have been of continuing importance in modern theological discussion.

I have made this selection not only for those who have a professional interest in the study of theology (clergy and ministers, teachers, students) but also for the interested member of the general public who, whether believer or not, wishes to have a guide to a reading of some important phases of twentieth-century theology. A general introduction attempts to set the scene and for each author there is a biographical note and brief introductions to the selected passages. In each case also there are suggestions for further study and reading.

University of Leeds   JOHN TINSLEY

INTRODUCTION TO THE SERIES

In this introductory chapter an attempt will be made to explain how the present theological situation in western Europe and the United States has come about. We shall trace very briefly the pedigree of contemporary ideas and attitudes. 'Theology' however is a word (like, e.g., 'mysticism', 'romanticism', 'philosophy') which is frequently and easily used without its meaning having first been made clear. It is not uncommon to find politicians and other public speakers using the word 'theology' to mean some recondite, antiquarian and hopelessly irrelevant intellectual pursuit involving, it is implied, a sad waste of mental energy. It is essential therefore to try first to clarify the meaning of the term 'theology'. A good way of doing this is to describe how theology is done. By describing the process of theology we shall more easily come to an understanding of what it essentially is.

Perhaps there have been as many attempts at a definition of theology as, for example, of art. The comparison with art is very relevant because theology is in one aspect, and a very important one, an instance of the perennial task of working with words to achieve lucidity and precision described by T. S. Eliot as 'the intolerable wrestle with words and meanings'. Even if we think we have found a more or less satisfactory language very often the cultural situation will have meantime so moved on that we find, in Eliot's words again, that we have only learned to get better words for the things we no longer want to say.

Nevertheless theologians have to keep on with this task not because they believe that it is possible, for instance, to describe 'God' or to find a language about God which is valid for all time, but because they believe that theology is a perennial human task. Man is a 'theologizing' animal: i.e., he must be constantly attempting to achieve in a significant pattern of words (or of words together with gestures and sound, as, for example, in liturgy) some way of rationalizing all those facets of his experience and history which point to a meaning beyond the visible and material. Because the most significant activity in religion, worship, involves among other things a particular use of language theology is, whether the fact be acknowledged by theologians or not, vitally linked with the arts and the problems raised by artistic creativity. Hence the amount of space taken up in this book with discussion of the nature of religious language, and the use of symbol, myth and metaphor in religion.

These subjects are of common interest to theologians and students of literature, and of the arts in general. The question of theology and language is however of special concern to the *Christian* theologian and the reason for this has never been better expressed than by St Augustine. In a famous passage in his *De Trinitate* he discusses the question why Christians should use trinitarian language when speaking about God. He is aware of the irritation and impatience of those who feel that theological language is attempting to make definitions precisely in a sphere where, in the nature of the case, such a thing is not possible. Augustine replies, however, that Christians have to be careful about language, especially language about God, *non ut diceretur sed ne taceretur*, which could be paraphrased 'not in order to define but because it is not possible just to say nothing'. Christians, of all people, cannot keep silence, adds Augustine, because God has broken silence in Christ and has spoken to mankind in him. We are bound therefore to make the best reply that we can.

More particularly theology invites comparison with what may properly be called the art of criticism, since it has the same relation to its subject matter (religion) as, for example, music criticism has to the symphony, art criticism to painting or sculpture, or literary criticism to poetry or prose. The best theology, like the best art, is that which so uses language that it sends the reader back with new and fruitful perspectives to the original (e.g., Christ, the Bible, etc.), or so speaks of the original that it affords a fresh and creative present experience of it.

Perhaps because of the great variety of approaches and methods possible for doing theology it is better, and here again the analogy from art is useful, not to think of what theology may be in the abstract but of actual types and styles of theology, and it is hoped that the selections given in this book will enable the reader to do this. The types and styles of theology are analogous to the types and styles of art. One could readily think in theology of the equivalents of, say, representational, impressionist, expressionist or abstract art. The 'quest of the historical Jesus' in the nineteenth century bears a resemblance to the 'pre-Raphaelite' school of painting in its attempt to portray Jesus in full and minute detail. Rudolf Bultmann and the 'existentialist' school of modern theology remind one of German 'expressionist' art where the subject of the painting is used as a means of expressing the commitment, feeling and attitudes of the artist. Further, like styles in art, theological styles continue to have significance even though they belong to an age now long past. The artist and the theologian are both in constant dialogue with their past traditions. To be a genuine contemporary, in both fields, means to have lived through, in imaginative experience, the outlook of previous practitioners. Theology belongs to the realm of human creativity and is therefore a dynamic and changing phenomenon. It is better, therefore, at the beginning of one's study of such a subject to look at the various methods of doing theology rather than to seek some distillation of it, some quintessential theology.

It would not be difficult to say something about what theology is from an analysis of the two words which make up the term theology—'theos' and 'logos'. Starting from these two components we might translate 'theology' as 'God-talk'. Theology as 'God-talk' takes its origin from two permanent features of human existence. There is first the fact that from time to time, in all sorts of ways, man finds himself wondering whether there is any meaning to his existence, whether the values and ideals which strike him in a cogent way in his many moral and aesthetic experiences are anything more than fine moments of feeling. There is further an impatience and a restlessness about human existence—we long for serenity, for wholeness and harmony, for unity and purpose, and continue to wonder whether in and behind material existence there is another order of reality.

These intimations of something beyond time and space have been variously expressed whether in the classical scheme of the values of 'truth, beauty and goodness', or in what Rudolf

Otto[1] has called the experience of the 'holy' or the 'numinous', or as far as aesthetic experience is concerned, in what Longinus[2] called the 'sublime'. Others have used the term 'mystery' for these features of human existence to express their sense of that which is mysterious, not in the way of a puzzle which is in principle solvable at some time or other, but as inducing, rather than the desire to solve, an overwhelming impression of awe, wonder, reverence, joy.

For the centre of this 'mystery' the Greek word would have been *theos,* sometimes translated 'god', but we may conveniently use it for any kind of transcendental reference given to human life. Man is a being who finds it difficult to undergo artistic, religious, scientific or moral experience and leave it just like that. He finds himself involved necessarily in the task of shaping this experience into significant patterns, trying to hold it in words or in some visual form. More particularly he is prompted to speech about it, to try and contain this experience in sentences. It is to this necessary use of language to analyse and explain *theos* that one can give the Greek word *logos.* Theology is, therefore, strictly speaking *theos-logos*— 'God-talk'. Theology results from the fact that on the one hand there is the 'mystery' and on the other the impulse to achieve understanding of it.

It is significant that many theologians have expressed a similar impatience with their task to that which we find in poets. We have already referred to Augustine and T. S. Eliot on the difficulties and frustrations of finding satisfactory words. This raises an important issue. Most frequently when we use the term 'theology' we think, inevitably and rightly, of verbal theology: that analysis of the 'mystery' of existence, that articulation of *theos* which can be done in words (*logos*). No doubt one would have to say that the best theology is that which approximates most closely to the character of its subject-matter. In the case of Christian theology this would mean the character of the Incarnation especially its 'signful', indirect, ambiguous, parabolic quality. Perhaps a more adequate kind of theology, a more satisfactory response to the *theos,* is that

[1] *The Idea of the Holy,* 1923.

[2] Cassius Longinus, Greek philosopher and critic of third century A.D., author of a treatise on literary criticism, *On the sublime.*

expressed in a concrete but non-verbal way in the arts, particularly the visual arts. If this is the case we ought to coin a new word for this reaction to *theos*. It would be a question not of *theos* and *logos* (=*verbal* theology) but of *theos* and *poiesis* ('making')—'theo-poetics'. The use of such a term as 'theo-poetics' would remind one of the saying of W. B. Yeats, specially appropriate to the Christian religion, that man cannot know the truth or express it in words. He can only *embody* (perhaps one could say 'incarnate') it. Even if we must continue to use the word 'theology' we need to think of it as a perennial attempt to *embody* human experience of *theos* rather than to translate it into some prose paraphrase.

This analysis of the meaning of the word 'theology' is a start, but it does not take us very far. We need to examine more closely how theologians have set about the task of 'God-talk', and the data which they have taken to be relevant. We must therefore turn to a brief review of what theologians have been doing during the last two centuries. This will help us to understand the theological scene today, and to recognize more clearly some of the 'styles' being used by theologians at the present time.

1

A radical change came over the method of doing Christian theology in the eighteenth century. Up till then, broadly speaking, and certainly from the time when theology had been given its most comprehensive and systematic expression in the works of St Thomas Aquinas (*c.* 1225–74) the procedure had seemed straightforward and uncomplicated. The scheme of theological investigation had two main parts: (1) natural theology and (2) revealed theology.

To take the method of doing 'natural' theology first. It was thought possible to establish by the ordinary processes of human reasoning such great truths as the existence of God and the immortality of the soul. Furthermore the ordinary processes of argumentation could establish the truth of certain attributes of God, like his omnipotence and omnipresence. From the evidence provided by the natural world and human existence it was possible to establish the existence of God by 'proofs'. The existence of God could be demonstrated by the use of unaided human reason. This was a truth about God open to any enquirer and could therefore rightly be called 'natural' theology.

'Revealed' theology was an important supplement to this. It had two additional functions to those performed by natural theology. First of all it conveyed again the truths of natural theology but this time in a 'revealed' form (particularly in the Christian scriptures) which could be readily and easily understood by those who were not able to follow rational argument. Then, second, revealed theology presented truths which could not be demonstrated by human reason, such as, for instance, the trinitarian nature of God. The scriptures attested the divinity of Christ by showing that he fulfilled Old Testament prophecy and worked miracles. These were taken to be the two foundations of belief in the authority of Christ. They established his place in the Christian revelation.

There were thus two kinds of data at the disposal of the theologian, natural theology and revealed theology, or to put it shortly 'reason' and 'revelation'. From an investigation of the book of nature and the book of scripture the theologian could construct an integrated and systematic theology, like the *Summa Theologiae* of St Thomas Aquinas. This was the general pattern of Christian apologetics commonly accepted until comparatively recently, and has remained the official view of the matter in the Roman Catholic Church. This method of doing theology was enshrined in William Paley's *View of the Evidences of Christianity* (1794) which remained in use as a text-book until as late as the beginning of the present century. Various criticisms had been brought against this way of doing theology before the advent of modern developments in philosophy, the sciences, and in biblical criticism. Reformation theology in general was suspicious of the large claims made by natural theology for the use of man's 'unaided' reason. Not only did the Reformers insist on the fact that all reasoning is undergirded by grace but they questioned whether one could say that human reason, even when so supported, inevitably attained the truths of natural theology. This seemed to them to neglect the problem of 'fallen' human nature which is capable

of perverting and corrupting even the process of reasoning.
During the eighteenth century the unsatisfactory character of
this traditional approach to theology became clearer still.
Many Christian apologists in this period tried to develop a
natural theology not by reading off from the book of nature
but by searching, so to speak, the book of man's inner experience. This seemed to show that there was among human beings
a general religious sense which lay behind all formally organized religions. So-called 'revealed' theology was therefore
taken to be simply a sophisticated articulation of this universal
natural theology. In this way the distinction between natural
and revealed theology was blurred, to say the least. Christianity,
for example, was seen not as a blend of natural and revealed
theology but a particular version of the universal feeling for
religion. To quote from the title of a book by a famous
eighteenth-century Deist, Matthew Tindal, it was as 'old as
creation ', nothing more than 'a republication of the religion
of nature'.

More dramatic in their effects on the traditional scheme of
theology, however, were the developments in scientific investigation and historical criticism which gathered momentum during the eighteenth century and continued apace throughout the
nineteenth century.

2

Research in the natural sciences during the nineteenth century,
especially in the fields of geology and biology, produced a
picture of the origin of the universe and its evolution radically
different from that suggested by a literal acceptance of the
early chapters of Genesis with a universe created in six days
and an Adam and Eve as the first human beings. *The Bridge-
water Treatises* (1833–40) showed, among other things, that it
was quite impossible, from the evidence already made available by geological research, to subscribe to the view that Creation could be exactly dated, as Archbishop Ussher[1] had

[1] James Ussher (1581–1656), Archbishop of Armagh, worked out a
complete biblical chronology in his *Annales Veteris et Novi Testamenti*,
and the dates given in this book were inserted in editions of the
Authorised Version of the Bible from 1701 onwards.

suggested, in 4004 B.C. For those who had been brought up on the idea that the Bible was itself the revelation of God, giving infallible truth as a series of propositions, this suggestion that the earth was millions rather than thousands of years old came as quite a shock. As late as 1851 John Ruskin could write: 'If only the geologists would let me alone, I could do very well, but those dreadful hammers! I hear the clink of them at the end of every cadence of the Bible verses.'

Following hard upon this shock came the news from the field of biological research. Charles Darwin's *The Origin of Species* was published in 1859 and his *The Descent of Man* in 1871. These made it clear not only that human life had evolved from sub-human species but that the whole process had been inconceivably longer than was generally supposed. Again for those brought up on the view that the Bible was a monolithic structure infallible on all subjects, including the science of human origins, this came as a great blow.

These shocks from outside the sphere of the Bible coincided with developments within biblical criticism which at the time seemed to undermine still further the status of the Bible as authoritative Scripture. As a result of literary and historical study it was no longer possible to maintain that the biblical literature was all of one kind, and all on the same level of authority or 'inspiration'. To take the Bible as an infallible oracle, to believe that in it the Word of God took print, was now seen to violate the nature of the biblical literature itself and to presuppose that the divine method of revelation is one which imposes rather than elicits, 'explains' rather than indicates, and forces rather than persuades.

Faced with these developments there were three possible reactions from Christian apologists. One could first simply refuse to recognize that any change had taken place and to carry on using the Bible as before, if anything hardening one's ideas about its authority and inerrancy. This is the approach which later on came to have the label 'fundamentalism' attached to it. Or, secondly, the attempt could be made to reconcile the new developments in knowledge with the traditional structure of theology. This was often taken to quite fantastic lengths like, for example, suggesting that the real significance of fossils in no way turned out to be a contradiction of the traditional dating of creation since they had been placed there by God to test faith! Similarly one remembers the notorious attempts to reconcile evolution with the scheme of creation in Genesis. Since the psalmist says that one day in the sight of the Lord is as a thousand years, 'days' in the Genesis account does not mean twenty-four hours but whatever extended period of time may be necessary to fit the case! Or, thirdly, one could accept the findings of research and in the light of them discard previous views of, for example, biblical inerrancy and look entirely afresh at the whole concept of revelation and the nature of the biblical literature. It was this latter reaction that has come to be known as nineteenth-century liberalism. Its main features were as follows.

First, a suspicion of the traditional schemes of dogmatic theology, and an attempt to reconstruct Christian belief in a way which took into account historical criticism. This could be illustrated by new procedures in such areas as christology or the doctrine of the Church. The traditional belief about the Christ as true God and true man, with two natures divine and human, as expressed in the traditional formula of the Council of Chalcedon 451 was put on one side, and an attempt made to construct a way of believing in Christ taking into account the results of historical criticism of the gospels, particularly the growing conviction that the fourth gospel, which had been a principal source for the formulation of traditional christology, was so much later than the synoptic gospels and so much less historical that it ought not to be used again in this way. The enigmatical Christ of the synoptic gospels, only indirectly indicating the meaning of himself, became the basis for a 'kenotic' christology. That is to say it was emphasized that whatever else the Incarnation was it meant an act of self-giving on the part of God which involved sacrificial self-limitation Or again one could take the doctrine of the Church, especially in its relation to Christ. In the light of biblical and historical criticism it was felt by many nineteenth-century scholars that the Christ of history, the genuine Jesus of Nazareth, was one thing, and the Christ of Church doctrine quite another. It seemed to be self-evident that the historical Christ could not have intended the Church as an institution, but rather that he was an outstanding Hebrew prophet who was concerned with brotherly love, justice, and the inestimable worth of the human soul.

The second characteristic of nineteenth-century liberalism was the use made of the category of evolution, provided by developments in the biological sciences. Human history was seen in terms of evolutionary progress. Mankind was seen to be, indubitably, on the march of progress. By the use of reason and the intellectual tools at his disposal man would be able to fashion a better future for himself. 'Sin', if the word were used at all, ought to be put in inverted commas and translated to mean imperfection or ignorance. 'Salvation' consequently ought to be thought of in terms of education and enlightenment. Such biblical concepts as 'the kingdom of God' ought similarly to be reinterpreted in terms of some kind of evolutionary progressivism.

Out of all this came some new principles for theological method and the data to be used by theology. The Bible remained as a principal source for the Christian theologian but it had to be used critically in the light of the findings of literary and historical investigation. The Bible also needed to be detached from its traditional interpretation in the church. In particular allegorization and typology were discarded as both inappropriate and irrelevant to such a critical use of the Bible. The book of the universe, nature, was also a source to be used, especially since it provided such a category of interpretation as evolutionary development. Finally there was increasing use of human experience as a source for theology. Nineteenth-century theology was greatly influenced by the work of Friedrich Schleiermacher (1768–1834) who considered the essence of the religious sentiment to be the feeling of absolute dependence and interpreted Christ as the supreme example of such dependence and 'God-consciousness'.

As far as relations with philosophy were concerned it has to be remembered that in the nineteenth century the task of philosophy was taken to be, principally, to provide a 'metaphysics', that is an all-embracing interpretation of the universe and human existence. The philosopher was one who concerned himself with what Tillich (see Vol. 3, pp. 73 ff.) called the 'ultimate questions of human existence'. The theologian's task was to keep on the look-out for philosophical schemes whose general outlook and vocabulary seemed to be particularly well-suited for the exposition of Christian beliefs. It was widely held during the nineteenth century, both on the Continent and in Britain, that such a congenial philosophical system had been found in the work of Friedrich Hegel (1770–1831). Hegel believed that existence could best be interpreted in terms of an evolutionary process, continually advancing from thesis to antithesis and fresh synthesis, whereby the Absolute Idea realized itself in ever more sharply focused ways. Adapting Christian trinitarian language he thought of the eternal Idea as God the Father. The eternal Idea as constantly passing from infinitude to finitude he thought of as God the Son. The Absolute Idea returning home, so to speak, enriched by this outgoing (Incarnation) he identified with the Christian God the Holy Spirit.

3

This was the background against which we can place all the theological movements represented in this series. Paul Tillich has described himself as a nineteenth-century figure, and certainly his concept of the relation between theology and philosophy as a 'correlation' (see Vol. 3, pp. 39 ff.) makes him very much more akin to the philosophy of the last century than to the analytical anti-metaphysical philosophy which has dominated the academic scene in twentieth-century Britain. Karl Barth's theological thinking began as a strong reaction against the liberal theology of the nineteenth-century and particularly its alliance with philosophies which he believed prevented the unique and distinctive features of the Christian religion from being clearly expressed. Bultmann took up the issues raised by the development of biblical criticism in the nineteenth century, particularly the question of the relation between the Jesus of history and the Christ of faith. Bonhoeffer in his early period shared Barth's reaction to nineteenth-century theology but later came to believe that a quite new situation faces the twentieth-century Christian and that Barth was of decreasing usefulness to such a person. Niebuhr's theology of politics and society is a deliberate reaction to a liberal theology which he believed had seriously underplayed the doctrines of sin and original sin and had placed an ultimate trust in human intelligence and virtue. We now need to examine more fully the place in the history of twentieth-century theology likely to be occupied by these five theologians.

All five of them were German or, in the case of Niebuhr, of German origin. As it happens they were also all of clerical or academic households. Further they all had experienced the age of Nazism and in most cases had suffered from it in one way or another.

The beginning of the theological movement associated with the name of *Karl Barth* can be dated from his shocked realization that the values of nineteenth-century liberalism as held by academics and intellectuals of his day left them incapable of recognizing tyranny when it appeared, much less of standing up against it. Academic education, even in theology, did not make men any more able to perceive the illiberalism and aggression implicit in the German policies which led to the outbreak of the 1914–18 war (see Vol. 1, pp. 36 ff.). The same inability of the liberal mind to believe in the recalcitrant and anti-rational possibilities of human conduct displayed itself again when the Nazis came to power in 1934. The theological charter which became the rallying point of church resistance to Hitler, the Barmen declaration, was mainly the work of Barth.

Certainly nothing could be more contrary to the theological method of nineteenth-century liberalism than that promulgated by Barth. For him the theological endeavour begins not with a series of questionings about human existence or the universe but by a realization that man is first confronted by an answer, a divine answer in the form of a revelation to which a unique witness is borne by the Bible. 'Religion' as the human enquiry after God, the human endeavour to attain God by the exercise of human reason is anathema to Barth (see Vol. 1, pp. 56 ff.). It is impossible for man to take any initiative, strictly speaking, in his enquiries about God because by his very existence man is a potential recipient of a revelation which is one of the inescapable givennesses of life. God is essentially a prevenient God who has first spoken to man, and anything that man says, any enquiry that he may make, must necessarily take the form of a response to a God who has all the while been addressing him. This is a method of doing theology directly opposed to that of Paul Tillich who begins his theology precisely with human questions, the 'ultimate questions' posed by human existence.

This starting point led Barth to place a new kind of emphasis on the Bible and the place of scripture in the formation of dogmatic theology. This started a movement which later on came to be known as 'biblical theology'. The Bible was regarded as providing the categories for Christian theology. Barth's theology has been given different names. One of them, his own term, is 'kerygmatic' theology, namely a theology which has first and foremost to be proclaimed. It is not sensible to argue about revelation Barth believed; one can only proclaim it.

There is also in Barth a new emphasis on the indissoluble links between theology and the church. Academic theology in the nineteenth century, especially in Germany, was separated from the life of the Church and the work of the pastor. The Church as the believing community came to have a new meaning for Barth as the body which finds itself bearing the Word of God and being judged by it.

Barth's way of doing Christology, of tackling the problems raised by the person of Christ, seems at first sight to be very much in the traditional manner. He began from the traditional formulation of the Council of Chalcedon of Christ as true God and true man. But he soon showed himself to be suspicious of the historical method of the nineteenth-century 'quest of the historical Jesus'. Barth suspected that this really made faith dependent on the results of historical investigation and practically equivalent to acceptance of an agreed amount of reliable factual information about Christ. It is instructive at this point to compare Barth's attitude to the historical Jesus with that of Bultmann, Tillich and Bonhoeffer. Barth treated more creatively and fruitfully than the nineteenth century the question of *kenosis* (self-emptying) in the Incarnation. This was not for Barth a matter of some loss of divinity, a downgrading of God. The *kenosis* in Christ is in fact the highest affirmation of the lordship of God over all. God is lord not only in transcendent glory but even in the form of the servant. God is free to be other personalities without ceasing to be himself. Whereas for so many 'kenotic' theologians in the nineteenth (and indeed twentieth centuries) the Incarnation had meant God revealing himself in a very qualified and impoverished way, for Barth the Incarnation is the expression (the Word) of a God who always had man, and the glorification of man in mind. God in Christ revealed his majesty precisely in the humiliations, trials and sufferings of Christ which many theologians in the past had thought must conceal it.

The resulting shape of Barth's theological scheme gives central place to the Incarnation, Scripture, and the Church. All Christian theology turns out in the end, according to Barth, to be an aspect of Christology whether it be the doctrine of creation, or of the church, or of the sacraments.[1]

Barth may have been neo-Calvinist in his approach to the doctrine of man, emphasizing human impotence before God, but in the end his theology of man turns out to be more optimistic than, say, that of Tillich or Niebuhr. There is a warm glow about Barth's language when he writes about man as he is in Christ, re-created man. On the other hand his theology is distanced from cultural and social interests. Barth saw what he called a *diastasis,* a tension between theology and the arts where Tillich perceived the possibilities of 'correlation'.

For *Bultmann* too the 1914–18 war was a turning point. It was during this period that he was working as a New Testament scholar on the form-critical method (see Vol. 2, pp. 37 ff.) and this proved to be determinative for his later work. He was sceptical about being able to get behind the 'kerygmatic' Christ of the gospels and sure that we do not have data for providing informed discussion about such subjects as the motivation of Christ or the self-awareness about his own mission. As well as the influence of Bultmann's scholarly investigations we need to reckon with his deep interest in the problem of communication, and his concern with the pastoral problems created by the fact that the tradition about Jesus comes down to us in a 'mythological' form. The extent of this problem was brought home to him by what he heard from army chaplains in the Second World War about their experiences in trying to preach and teach. This raised in an acute form the whole

[1] *Church Dogmatics,* 1, 2, pp. 123 ff.

question of how the Christian gospel is to be communicated in the modern world. This involved a study of the status of 'mythology' in the Christian religion. Is it an essential form of human speech, or it is accidental, temporary, continually replaceable by more satisfactory translations or paraphrases into other kinds of language? Bultmann came to believe the latter and hence insisted upon the need for 'demythologizing' (see Vol. 2, pp. 64 ff.).

Bultmann took over the language of 'existentialist' philosophy as that which is specially well equipped to express the kind of religious belief we find in the New Testament. 'Existentialist' thinking is that in which we are ourselves personally involved, the kind of thinking in which we are personally implicated. It calls for personal decision and genuine commitment. Existentialism is antipathetic to any philosophy which is merely theoretical or academic (in the bad sense). The debate started by Bultmann's transposition of New Testament belief into existentialist terms has centred on whether this emphasis on the subjective, on *my* decision and commitment here and now, is adequate to do justice to the many facets of Christianity. Is not the New Testament also concerned with certain objective facts, like the redemption wrought by Christ, which remain true irrespective of any personal decision and commitment. Sometimes after reading a lot of Bultmann one has the feeling that when the existentialist theologian says 'God' he really means 'me'. Or at least it sounds like that!

Bultmann shares the hesitations of Barth about exposing the Incarnation to the ambiguities and probabilities of historical investigation. This would make faith vulnerable to the hazards of historical criticism and Bultmann, like Barth, seems intent on finding some area for faith which is immune from that eventuality.

So the data for theology which is to determine one's starting point is not the world, nor is it the Bible in the way Barth takes it, although the New Testament plays a cardinal role in Bultmann's theology. Rather it is human existence, because this is where the whole question of faith is posed. The mythological idiom of the New Testament really relates to man in his existential predicaments, to the need for decision, and for turning from 'inauthentic' to 'authentic' existence.

When we turn to *Paul Tillich* we find a theologian who is very much closer than Barth or Bultmann to the liberal tradition and to principles of liberal investigation. Tillich's whole approach to theology is based on the assumption that man has a natural ability to apprehend truth and that there is in man 'a depth of reason'. He starts from anthropology, examining the implications of the questions which are set by human existence.

Tillich agreed with Barth that theology is 'kerygmatic' but he insisted that it is also 'apologetic'. He kept a place for 'natural theology'. If theology is treated as only 'kerygmatic' Tillich believed, and I think rightly, that it then becomes irrelevant outside the domestic circle of believers, and is only useful for 'revivalism', as he put it.

Tillich departed radically from Bultmann on the question of myth and symbol. 'Demythologizing' for Tillich was an impossible enterprise because the myth is by its very nature irreplaceable and untranslatable, and cannot be transposed into a paraphrase without serious distortion or reduction. 'Myth' is a significant pattern of symbols organized into a narrative story which has the peculiar power, whenever it is receptively read or heard of bringing with it a clearer perception and deeper understanding of some feature of human experience which can not be evoked or expressed in any other way. Tillich believed that myth was therefore fundamentally irreplaceable. Bultmann on the other hand does not see myth existing in its own permanent right, but rather as a temporary way of putting things in a certain culture, which may now be seen perhaps as striking and picturesque, but not a necessary form of human speech.

Tillich was outstanding among the group represented in this series, and indeed in the twentieth century generally, for the attention he gave to analysing the relation between theology and culture. On this issue he was far removed from Barth and closer to a thinker like Niebuhr.

Reinhold Niebuhr's work can also be seen as a reaction against the preceding liberal theology. He is specially critical of the tendencies in nineteenth-century theology to equate the 'kingdom of God' with social betterment or progress. His theological endeavour could be described as an essay in 'prophetic realism'. He sought, that is to say, to relate biblical insights into the meaning of history and God's judgement on and in it to the political and social situation of his day. His aim was 'realism' in the sense that he had a deep suspicion of what one American writer has called 'the men of the infinite', that is the idealists, the romantics, the men of abstract generalization. Niebuhr preferred the company of 'the men of the finite', those with a careful eye for data, evidence, facts. A good example of this 'prophetic realism' is to be found in the essay 'The ultimate trust' in *Beyond Tragedy*.

Like Tillich, but unlike Barth, Niebuhr starts from the human situation. Here again one finds his work a marked contrast to nineteenth-century liberalism in the way he expounds afresh the doctrines of the 'fall of man' and 'original sin', and the place he gives to eschatology. The basic form of sin for Niebuhr is not finitude or imperfection but the anxiety about them which human freedom makes possible and which expresses itself in pride and envy.

Niebuhr takes up from liberal theology the results of biblical criticism, especially as it affects biblical history. 'Fundamentalist' approaches to the Bible blurred the distinction between different literary forms, and, most disastrously, between symbolic language and language of historical fact.

The theology of *Bonhoeffer*, fragmentary though it be, is of the greatest importance in showing a man struggling to free himself from various traditions in his early training notably the influence of Karl Barth, and re-cast the whole structure of theology to face a new situation. Bonhoeffer came to believe that the theology of Barth and Bultmann had seriously neglected the social and political problems of the world. In this respect he found the theology of Niebuhr, which he came to know well as a result of his visits to America, very much more congenial.

Bonhoeffer was very much concerned with the significance of Christ, and especially the place of the historical Christ in Christian belief. His theology is, in one respect, an attempt to reconstruct a Christocentric theology and ethics just as thoroughgoing in its Christocentricity as Barth's. He does not, however, isolate the place and role of the Bible in the manner of Barth nor does he put the whole stress on inwardness in the existentialist fashion of Bultmann and Tillich.

4

The theologians represented in this series are already established figures on the twentieth-century theological scene, and their writings have by now attained the status of 'classics'. What developments have there been among a younger genera- of theologians? Recently a number of new movements have come into vogue which could be given the labels: 'The new theology', 'Secular Christianity' and 'The death of God theology'. There is space here only for a brief word about each of these developments.

One of the most astonishing phenomena in recent years has been the popular success of Dr John A. T. Robinson's *Honest to God*, first published in 1963, which has now sold well over one million copies, as well as being translated into a great number of foreign languages. The extraordinary circulation of this book is strange because it was not written for a popular audience, it contains long extracts from Tillich, Bultmann and Bonhoeffer which make severe demands on the general reader, and it could not be described as a piece of creative or lucid theological writing. The author would be the first to say that he was not attempting a new theology but to promote a discussion of the three thinkers just mentioned who had hitherto, especially in this country, been known only by academics and professional theologians. It was perhaps the tone of voice of this book rather than its contents which gave it such popular appeal particularly since the author was a bishop, with all that the image of such a person still implies in this country. The picture which the book suggested of a bishop not pontificating theological certainties in dogmatizing fashion, but exploring in a very tentative way and voicing his own doubts and uncertainties, struck a new note for many people. *Honest to God* appeared to be the manifesto of a movement of liberation, and to express the feeling that belief was a continuous dialogue with doubt within each person, and not an unchangeable certainty over against the unbelief of others.

Many critics have pointed out the obscurities and confusions in Dr Robinson's book. One of these is significant and worth pausing over. This is the question of the place and function of metaphor in religious language which he brings up in the first chapter on the God 'up there or out there'. He expresses his irritation with this kind of language but without making it at all clear what he takes a phrase like 'God is up there' to mean. If he is arguing that God is not 'up there' in the sense that God is not an entity that one could theoretically examine in, say, the course of space exploration, this is an assertion not to be found in traditional Christian theology. There is, however, a sense in which it is most true to say that God is 'up there' or 'out there' and that is that 'God' is not simply another word for human life or experience at its most profound or intense. It is not clear, on this basic issue, which of the two uses the bishop has in mind.

This is a very significant area of confusion and it pinpoints what is a real situation of crisis in contemporary theology. This is 'the crisis of metaphor', and it bears on the discussions about 'myth' and symbolism to be found in a number of the extracts given in this series. Man as a finite being is bound to be a metaphor-making animal so long as he experiences intimations of realities outside or beyond what can be measured scientifically. This means, at the least, so long as he remains capable of aesthetic, moral, and mystical experience. The fact, for instance, that to indicate these experiences he uses the spatial language of a 'three-decker' universe ('up there', 'down there') is not the 'scandal' that Bultmann and Dr Robinson take it to be. This is a serious misplacing of what is the real 'stumbling-block' for twentieth-century man as far as Christian language is concerned. In fact the 'three-decker' universe is not a bad image to use in any talk about values and religious beliefs, at least for finite man in a space-time universe which is likely to be the condition of most of mankind in the foreseeable future. For spaceless man no doubt another image would be necessary, but until it is demonstrated that spacelessness is to be the permanent human state to try and dispense with spatial or temporal metaphor or even to be coy about its use is not a sign of maturity or progress. It indicates an inhuman and senseless attempt to try and jump out of our finite skin. The momentum of the human mind, as the poet Wallace Stevens put it, is towards abstraction. Part of the appeal of a 'demythologized' version of Christianity, suggested by Bultmann and others, and commended by Dr Robinson, is that it takes one away from the trying particularities of the concrete. But 'concretization', to use Bonhoeffer's term, is a necessary undertaking for the Christian religion as long as it is firmly rooted in an historical and particular Incarnation. It is this feature of the Christian religion which indicates where the real 'stumbling-block' for modern man has to be placed. This is precisely where St Paul put it, in the enigmatical ambiguity of a Christ who is so identified with the human scene as to be, seemingly, indistinguishable from it, except to the eyes of faith.

It would be generally true to say that all the theologians represented in this series took a view about the task of philosophy which has now become very unfashionable in Britain. They believed the job of the philosopher was to build up a world-view, a 'metaphysics'. Both Barth and Tillich shared this view. Barth suspected that the very 'world-view' inherent in philosophy would blur the distinctiveness of Christianity. Bultmann believed that 'existentialism' provided a coherent 'metaphysics' of human existence. Niebuhr and the earlier Bonhoeffer approached philosophy in the same way.

It is the special interest of Paul van Buren's *The Secular Meaning of the Gospel* (1963) that it discusses the relation between Christian theology and the type of linguistic or analytical philosophy which has developed in Britain and the United States. For philosophers like Ludwig Wittgenstein, G. E. Moore and A. J. Ayer the task of the philosopher is not to construct a 'world-view' but to analyse and classify language. The philosopher studies how language works and the meanings which we attach to statements. He seeks to establish ways of verifying the truth of the various assertions we make.

In the first wave of linguistic analysis popularized by A. J. Ayer's *Language, Truth and Logic* (1936) it was asserted that the only kind of language which had meaning was that which was scientifically verifiable. All other types of language, poetry, for example, or moral exhortation or religion, were said to be meaningless because they were not susceptible to this kind of verification. Philosophical linguistic analysis has modified this position in recent years, and the concern now is how to classify the uses of language and to discuss the types of meaning appropriate to each in relation to the contexts in which they are used.

Paul van Buren seeks to relate the exposition of Christian theology to this kind of linguistic philosophical analysis. Also he has in mind the wish expressed by Bonhoeffer that one ought to be seeking for a 'non-religious interpretation' of biblical and theological concepts. van Buren's book has been nicknamed 'The case of the disappearing gospel'. Certainly in the process of re-stating Christianity in 'non-religious' language he so dissolves traditional Christian theology that it is difficult to see what if anything a believer of former times would recognize in it as familiar.

In *The Secular Meaning of the Gospel* van Buren contended that there is a residual Christianity, even when one has abandoned the idea that any meaning can be attached to 'God' or the 'transcendent'. This remainder he turns into a kind of moral heroism. Christ becomes for all men a model, *the* paradigm, of 'openness' and freedom. The significance of Christ is that he has shown himself, and continues to show himself to be a potent example of these qualities.

The most recent phase of theology has been called the 'death of God' movement. This is the title of a book by Gabriel Vahanian, and it has been used to describe the work not only of Vahanian but of Thomas Altizer (*The Gospel of Christian Atheism*) and William Hamilton, *The Essence of Christianity*.

If one complained about confusion in *Honest to God* this complaint would have to be brought even more sharply against some of these theologians, especially Altizer, whose work is irritatingly rhapsodic just at the points where clarity of expression is most required. It is not at all easy to be sure of what exactly is being said. In one way Altizer seems to be saying that Nietzsche's cry, 'God is dead', still needs repeating, particularly since as far as modern man in a technological society is concerned belief in God as a transcendent reality upon whom mankind depends has no meaning, and is hopelessly irrelevant. Man must now look to his own resources as he prepares to take charge of his own evolution.

Another side of Altizer seems to be saying, again in a very

confused way, that Christians have been reluctant to come to realistic terms with the Incarnation, particularly with its corollary that Christ really died the death. This is a useful point because it is true that Christians have traditionally not only denied that Christ was born in the way that we are, but there remained for a long time in Christian theology, especially in the Greek church, the belief that Christ's human flesh was not mortal flesh as ours is.

Altizer wishes to press the reality of the *kenosis* or self-giving in Incarnation so that one can say with Charles Péguy, 'God too has faced death'. But Altizer seems to take *kenosis* to mean a literal self-annihilation. He speaks of the death of God as 'an historical event'. If these words mean anything Altizer is saying that in the Incarnation God, as it were, committed suicide. The death of God in Christ has freed us to become our own Christs, the result of the Incarnation being that God has diffused himself in the human race. This sounds like a new version of pantheism.

What is specially interesting in the 'death of God' theologians is the place which they are still willing to accord to Christ. In spite of form-criticism and the wave of scepticism which it produced both Altizer and Hamilton seem to believe that there is sufficiently reliable information available about Jesus to warrant our thinking again about the ideal of the 'imitation of Christ'. This is interpreted along very different lines from Bonhoeffer's presentation of the *imitatio Christi*. It reminds one of what Kierkegaard called 'admiration of Christ', a heroic endeavour to reproduce his 'openness' and 'freedom' by sheer effort of will.

5

It is hazardous to suggest what is likely to be the prospect for theology in the rest of this century. However, it seems to me that four areas will provide material for special clarification : (1) There is first what I have called the 'crisis of metaphor' in modern theology. Theology and religious language stand or fall by metaphor and all that it implies about human life and human perception. The impulse to metaphor, to speak of one

thing in terms of another, prompts the question whether the
relation between appearance and reality may not be of the kind
which religious belief suggests. The surrender of metaphor
means the end of religion and, significantly, the death of what
we have come to regard as distinctively human feelings. The
French 'anti-novelist' Alain Robbe-Grillet is perfectly right to
detect an important link between metaphor and religion.
Robbe-Grillet wishes to get rid of metaphor because it implies
some hidden relationship between man and the universe, and
this takes us half-way to religion. Indeed, there is a 'crisis of
metaphor' in modern literature as well as in modern theology.
Bultmann can speak disparagingly of 'mere metaphors' and
advocates 'demythologization' because myth, metaphor and
symbol can be taken in a crude literal way, or can become
obsolete. These are certainly hazards in the human situation,
which often necessitate a drastic process of unlearning. But a
worse fate, a greater hurt to the soul is to attempt to bring
about a state of affairs where such hazards are no longer
possible. It is damaging either to identify metaphor and
actuality or to romanticize pantheistically (in a way that alarms
Robbe-Grillet), but it is worse to believe that as individuals and
as a generation we have gone beyond the need for metaphor.
At stake, therefore, in the present 'crisis of metaphor' in
literature and religion is nothing less than the humanization or
dehumanization of man.

(2) There needs to be very much more exploration of what
Tillich called 'correlation' between religion and the arts.
Christians have lived too long with the assumption that while
art may have aesthetic or pedagogical value, it is no serious
avenue to truth. Art has been regarded as useful for those who
cannot read, and need pictures, but not for the literate who
having mastered discursive reasoning and the manipulation of
abstractions have no need of the image. Art has therefore been
taken by many theologians to be inferior to philosophy, and
on the whole Christian theologians have preferred to cultivate
relations with philosophers rather than artists. This is, however,
to beg the question whether art is a way of knowing which is
as truth-bearing, in its way, as philosophical or scientific
method. Christians have surrendered with amazing ease to the
notion that the image is a lesser form of truth than the

concept, as if image and concept were simply alternative ways of saying the same thing, except that the image helps those who have more imagination than logic. It is arguable that the Christian religion would have gained as much (perhaps more) from association with art as it has from philosophy, not only for general apologetic reasons, but for intellectual arguments with what Schleiermacher called its 'cultural despisers'.

(3) Thirdly, there is the continuing work of interpreting afresh the significance of Christ and in the immediate future this will have to include a thorough exploration of what it means to talk about the uniqueness of Christ and his finality.

In spite of the central place which it occupies in the structure of their beliefs, it has proved persistently difficult for Christians to take the Incarnation with full realism and to follow through its implications in a rigorously realistic way. It took Christians a very long time indeed to accept the belief that the Incarnation meant taking a human biology exactly like ours. What a struggle there was in the early Church to get accepted the belief that Christ really died the death in the way that we do! The history of the iconography of the crucifixion in art shows that it took nearly five centuries before a body of Christ appeared on the cross, and then it is very much a live Christ who, eyes open, stands on the cross as a royal warrior looking through the scene. It took the Christian Church nearly ten centuries before a really dead body of Christ appeared on the cross, and even then it was not a death in suffering and agony. It is another century and a half before a bleeding, suffering emaciated Christ with a crown of thorns appears in the representation of the crucifixion. This is a long time, but it has taken Christians even longer to come anywhere near accepting that the Incarnation involved taking a genuine human psychology of the kind that might mean that Christ had to find his way to religious belief in exactly the same way as everybody else, through faith, through acting on signs which, because they are ambiguous and our freedom is real, can always be 'stumbling-blocks' ('scandals' in the New Testament) that offend. Just as dangerous as a theology based on the 'God of the gaps' has been a 'Christology of the gaps', that is, a tendency to insert a capacity for full divine self-awareness on

• •

the part of the historical Jesus in some 'gap' in his psyche, or, so it has sometimes been suggested, in his subconscious!

The question of the finality of Christ suggests the fourth area in which it is likely that theology will be specially engaged in the immediate future: comparative religion, and especially comparative theology.

(4) In the contemporary world it sometimes appears that the 'ecumenical' movement of unbelief grows faster than that of belief, so that all religions are finding themselves on the same side of the fence as far as faith that human life has a transcendental significance is concerned. In this situation there needs to be more conversation between the theologies of the religions, particularly those whose history gives them a special kinship: Judaism, Christianity and Islam. If the Christian has to start thinking again about the meaning of Incarnation and the unique place which he assigns to Christ there is no more bracing company in which he could explore this question than that of the Jew and Muslim.

The present-day student of the Christian doctrines of the Trinity and the Incarnation might well begin with reflection on the familiar strictures on these doctrines that come from the Jew and the Muslim: that they violate the concept of the unity of God, and, by involving God in human history in a finite way, blaspheme against the majesty of God. The Christian will want to have as rich a doctrine that God is one as the Jew or the Muslim, and that God is known in historical event, and perhaps this is now more likely to be attained by going to school theologically with these two religions. Further the three religions of Judaism, Christianity and Islam have much to give each other in working out afresh for our own day the meaning of what it is to be human. Bishop Kenneth Cragg has shown how profound a realization of the nature of man comes from relating the Jewish/Christian concept of man made in the 'image of God' to the Muslim concept of man as 'God's caliph'.

Much needs to be unlearned and relearned in this field. Judaism, Islam and Buddhism have suffered from misleading propagandist slogans in the past like 'Jewish legalism', 'Islam

---

[1] Kenneth Cragg, *The Privilege of Man*, London, 1968.

is the most materialistic and least religious of the religions',
'Buddhism is insensitive to suffering or social justice'. These
are Christian caricatures of the truth, and there is now a fresh
chance, especially in those western countries which are now
multi-religious, to rectify this distortion by mutual understanding in co-operative study.

BIOGRAPHICAL INTRODUCTION

Reinhold Niebuhr was born in 1892 in Wright City, Missouri, where his father Gustav Niebuhr was the German pastor. Like Tillich he paid warm tribute in later life to the influence of his father: 'The first formative religious influence on my life was my father, who combined a vital personal piety with a complete freedom in his theological studies.'

Niebuhr began his theological studies at Elmhurst College and theological seminary, and then graduated at the University of Yale. He was appointed pastor in Detroit in 1915 just at the time when the Ford Motor Company was beginning its spectacular expansion. His experiences at Detroit influenced him, Niebuhr said later, more than any of the books he had hitherto read. He became vividly aware 'of the irrelevance of the mild moralistic idealism, which I had identified with the Christian faith, to the power realities of our modern technical society'. His youthful optimism was undermined by the 'social realities of Detroit' and 'the moral pretensions of Henry Ford'. An entry in his journal for 1927 explains what he meant by this phrase:

The new Ford car is out. The town is full of talk about it. Newspaper reports reveal that it is the topic of the day in all world centers. Crowds storm every exhibit to get the first glimpse of this new creation. Mr. Ford has given out an interview saying that the car has cost him about a hundred million dollars and that after finishing it he still has about a quarter of a billion dollars in the bank.

I have been doing a little arithmetic and have come to the conclusion that the car cost Ford workers at least fifty million in lost wages during the past year. No one knows how many hundreds lost their homes in the period of unemployment, and how many children were taken out of school to help fill the depleted family exchequer, and how many more children lived on short rations during this period. Mr. Ford refuses to concede that he made a mistake in bringing the car out so late. He has a way of impressing the public even with his mistakes. We are now asked to believe that the whole idea of waiting a year after the old car stopped selling before bringing out a new one was a great advertising scheme which reveals the perspicacity of this industrial genius. But no one asks about the toll in human lives.

What a civilization is this ! Naïve gentlemen with a genius for mechanics suddenly become the arbiters over the lives and fortunes of hundreds of thousands. Their moral pretensions are credulously accepted at full value. No one bothers to ask whether an industry which can maintain a cash reserve of a quarter of a billion ought not to make some provision for its unemployed. It is enough that the new car is a good one. Here is a work of art in the only realm of art which we can understand. We will therefore refrain from making undue ethical demands upon the artist. Artists of all the ages have been notoriously unamenable to moral discipline. The cry of the hungry is drowned in the song, 'Henry has made a lady out of Lizzy'.[1]

Out of this experience came such books as *Moral Man and Immoral Society* (1932) and *The Nature and Destiny of Man* (1941). In 1928 Niebuhr was appointed Professor of Christian Ethics at Union Theological Seminary, New York, remaining there until his retirement in 1960. Niebuhr both as writer and speaker exercised great influence on social and religious thinking in both America and Britain especially during and after the Second World War. The poet W. H. Auden owed much in the development of his religious beliefs, especially about its social implications, to Reinhold Niebuhr and his wife Ursula to whom the volume *Nones* (1942) is dedicated.

Niebuhr died on 31 May 1971.

[1] *Leaves from the notebook of a tamed cynic* (entry for 1927), pp. 180–1.

SELECTIONS

1 MAN AS A PROBLEM TO HIMSELF

[One of the most memorable features of Niebuhr's writing is his exposition of the Christian concept of man. He is particularly skilful in striking a fine balance between those contradictory elements in man which make him as Pascal put it 'ni ange ni bête' (neither angel nor animal). This extract shows how the commonly accepted view of man in the West has been a blend of classical (especially Greek) and Judaeo-Christian traditions. He then characterizes these two traditions: the classical view, where man as made in the image of God is interpreted in terms of his rational capacity, and the Christian where the image of God is not a possession (like reason) but a relationship to God in which he may (or may not) wish to stand.]

Man has always been his own most vexing problem. How shall he think of himself? Every affirmation which he may make about his stature, virtue, or place in the cosmos becomes involved in contradictions when fully analysed. The analysis reveals some presupposition or implication which seems to deny what the proposition intended to affirm.

If man insists that he is a child of nature and that he ought not to pretend to be more than the animal which he obviously is, he tacitly admits that he is, at any rate, a curious kind of animal who has both the inclination and the capacity to make such pretensions. If on the other hand he insists upon his unique and distinctive place in nature and points to his rational faculties as proof of his special eminence, there is usually an anxious note in his avowals of uniqueness which betrays his unconscious sense of kinship with the brutes. This note of anxiety gives a poignant significance to the heat and animus in which the Darwinian controversy[1] was conducted

---

[1] The controversy about the evolution of human life, especially man's 'descent from the apes', which followed the publication of Charles Darwin's *The Origin of Species* (1859) and *The Descent of Man* (1871). (Ed.)

and the Darwinian thesis was resisted by the traditionalists. Furthermore the very effort to estimate the significance of his rational faculties implies a degree of transcendence over himself which is not fully defined or explained in what is usually connoted by 'reason'. For the man who weighs the importance of his rational faculties is in some sense more than 'reason', and has capacities which transcend the ability to form general concepts.

If man takes his uniqueness for granted he is immediately involved in questions and contradictions on the problem of his virtue. If he believes himself to be essentially good and attributes the admitted evils of human history to specific social and historical causes, he involves himself in begging the question; for all these specific historical causes of evil are revealed, upon close analysis, to be no more than particular consequences and historical configurations of evil tendencies in man himself. They cannot be understood at all if a capacity for, and inclination towards, evil in man himself are not presupposed. If, on the other hand, man comes to pessimistic conclusions about himself, his capacity for such judgements would seem to negate the content of the judgements. How can man be 'essentially' evil if he knows himself to be so? What is the character of the ultimate subject, the quintessential 'I', which passes such devastating judgements upon itself as object?

If one turns to the question of the value of human life and asks whether life is worth living, the very character of the question reveals that the questioner must in some sense be able to stand outside of, and to transcend, the life which is thus judged and estimated. Man can reveal this transcendence more explicitly not only by actually committing suicide, but by elaborating religions and philosophies which negate life and regard a 'lifeless' eternity, such as Nirvana,[1] as the only possible end of life.

Have those who inveigh so violently against otherworldliness in religion, justified as their criticisms may be, ever fully realized what the error of denying life implies in regard to the

[1] Nirvana, a sanskrit word meaning literally 'coolness' and denoting in Buddhism the state of equilibrium or non-attachment when one has learned how to be free from the clamorous demands of the self. (Ed.)

stature of man? The man who can negate 'life' must be something other than mere vitality. Every effort to dissuade him
from the neglect of natural vitality and historic existence
implies a vantage point in him above natural vitality and
history; otherwise he could not be tempted to the error from
which he is to be dissuaded.

Man's place in the universe is subject to the same antinomies. Men have been assailed periodically by qualms of
conscience and fits of dizziness for pretending to occupy the
centre of the universe. Every philosophy of life is touched with
anthropocentric tendencies. Even theocentric religions believe
that the Creator of the world is interested in saving man from
his unique predicament. But periodically man is advised and
advises himself to moderate his pretensions and admit that he
is only a little animal living a precarious existence on a second-
rate planet, attached to a second-rate sun. There are moderns
who believe that this modesty is the characteristic genius of
modern man and the fruit of his discovery of the vastness of
interstellar spaces; but it was no modern astronomer who confessed, 'When I consider thy heavens, the work of thy fingers,
the moon and the stars, which thou hast ordained; What is
man, that thou art mindful of him?' (Ps. 8:3–4). Yet the
vantage point from which man judges his insignificance is a
rather significant vantage point. This fact has not been lost on
the moderns, whose modesty before the cosmic immensity was
modified considerably by pride in their discovery of this
immensity. It was a modern, the poet Swinburne, who sang
triumphantly:

The seal of his knowledge is sure, the truth and his spirit are
wed; . . .

Glory to Man in the highest ! for man is the master of things,
thereby proving that the advance of human knowledge about
the world does not abate the pride of man.

While these paradoxes of human self-knowledge are not
easily reduced to simpler formulae, they all point to two facts
about man: one of them obvious and the other not quite as
obvious. The two are not usually appreciated with equal
sympathy. The obvious fact is that man is a child of nature,
subject to its vicissitudes, compelled by its necessities, driven

by its impulses, and confined within the brevity of the years
which nature permits its varied organic forms, allowing them
some, but not too much, latitude. The other less obvious fact
is that man is a spirit who stands outside of nature, life, himself, his reason and the world. This latter fact is appreciated
in one or the other of its aspects by various philosophies. But
it is not frequently appreciated in its total import. That man
stands outside of nature in some sense is admitted even by
naturalists who are intent upon keeping him as close to nature
as possible. They must at least admit that he is *homo faber*, a
tool-making animal. That man stands outside the world is
admitted by rationalists who, with Aristotle, define man as a
rational animal and interpret reason as the capacity for
making general concepts. But the rationalists do not always
understand that man's rational capacity involves a further
ability to stand outside himself, a capacity for selftranscen-
dence, the ability to make himself his own object, a quality of
spirit which is usually not fully comprehended or connoted in
'*ratio*' or '*nous*' or 'reason' or any of the concepts which
philosophers usually use to describe the uniqueness of man.

How difficult it is to do justice to both the uniqueness of
man and his affinities with the world of nature below him is
proved by the almost unvarying tendency of those philosophies,
which describe and emphasize the rational faculties of man or
his capacity for self-transcendence, to forget his relation to
nature and to identify him, prematurely and unqualifiedly,
with the divine and the eternal; and of naturalistic philosophies
to obscure the uniquesness of man.

THE CLASSICAL VIEW OF MAN

Though man has always been a problem to himself, modern
man has aggravated that problem by his too simple and premature solutions. Modern man, whether idealist or naturalist,
whether rationalist or romantic, is characterized by his simple
certainties about himself. He has aggravated the problem of
understanding himself because these certainties are either in
contradiction with each other or in contradiction with the

obvious facts of history, more particularly of contemporary history; and either they have been controverted by that history or they are held in defiance of its known facts. It is not unfair to affirm that modern culture, that is, our culture since the Renaissance, is to be credited with the greatest advances in the understanding of nature and with the greatest confusion in the understanding of man. Perhaps this credit and debit are logically related to each other.

Fully to appreciate the modern conflicts in regard to human nature it is necessary to place the characteristically modern doctrines of man in their historic relation to the traditional views of human nature which informed Western culture. All modern views of human nature are adaptations, transformations and varying compounds of primarily two distinctive views of man: (*a*) The view of classical antiquity, that is of the Graeco-Roman world, and (*b*) the Biblical view. It is important to remember that, while these two views are distinct and partly incompatible, they were actually merged in the thought of mediaeval Catholicism. (The perfect expression of this union is to be found in the Thomistic synthesis of Augustinian and Aristotelian thought.) The history of modern culture really begins with the destruction of this synthesis, foreshadowed in nominalism, and completed in the Renaissance and Reformation. In the dissolution of the synthesis, the Renaissance distilled the classical elements out of the synthesis and the Reformation sought to free the Biblical from the classical elements. Liberal Protestantism is an effort (on the whole an abortive one) to reunite the two elements. There is, in fact, little that is common between them. What was common in the two views was almost completely lost after modern thought had reinterpreted and transmitted the classical view of man in the direction of a greater naturalism. Modern culture has thus been a battleground of two opposing views of human nature. This conflict could not be resolved. It ended in the more or less complete triumph of the modernized classical view of man, a triumph which in this latter day is imperilled not by any external foe but by confusion within its own household. To validate this analysis of the matter requires at least a brief preliminary analysis of the classical and the Christian views of human nature.

The classical view of man, comprised primarily of Platonic, Aristotelian and Stoic conceptions of human nature, contains, of course, varying emphases, but it may be regarded as one in its common conviction that man is to be understood primarily from the standpoint of the uniqueness of his rational faculties. What is unique in man is his *nous*. *Nous* may be translated as 'spirit', but the primary emphasis lies upon the capacity for thought and reason. In Aristotle the *nous* is the vehicle of purely intellectual activity and is a universal and immortal principle which enters man from without. Only one element in it, the 'passive' in distinction to the 'active' *nous*, becomes involved in, and subject to, the individuality of a particular physical organism. How completely the Aristotelian *nous* is intellectual may best be understood by Aristotle's explicit denial of its capacity for self-consciousness. It does not make itself its own object except in making things known the object of consciousness: 'No mind knows itself by participation in the known; it becomes known by touching and knowing, so that the same thing is mind and object of mind.'[1] This definition is the more significant when contrasted with Aristotle's conception of divine consciousness which expresses itself only in terms of self-knowledge.

In Plato the *nous* or *logistikon* is not as sharply distinguished from the soul as in Aristotle. It is, rather, the highest element in the soul, the other two being the spirited element (θυμοειδές) and the appetitive element (ἐπιθυμητικόν). In both Plato and Aristotle 'mind' is sharply distinguished from the body. It is the unifying and ordering principle, the organ of *logos*, which brings harmony into the life of the soul, as *logos* is the creative and forming principle of the world. Greek metaphysical presuppositions are naturally determinative for the doctrine of man; and since Parmenides[2] Greek philosophy had on the one hand assumed an identity between being and reason and on the other had presupposed that reason works upon some formless or unformed stuff which is never completely tractable. In the thought of Aristotle matter is 'a remnant, the non-existent in itself unknowable and alien to reason, that remains

[1] *Physics*, 20.
[2] Parmenides, sixth to fifth century B.C., Greek philosopher. (Ed.)

after the process of clarifying the thing into form and conception. This non-existent neither is nor is not; it is "not yet", that is to say it attains reality only in so far as it becomes the vehicle of some conceptual determination.'[1]

Plato and Aristotle thus share a common rationalism, and also a common dualism which is explicit in the case of Plato and implicit and covert in the case of Aristotle.[2] The effect of this rationalism and dualism has been determinative for the classical doctrine of man and for all modern doctrines which are borrowed from it. The consequences are: (*a*) The rationalism practically identifies rational man (who is essential man) with the divine; for reason is, as the creative principle, identical with God. Individuality is no significant concept, for it rests only upon the particularity of the body. In the thought of Aristotle only the active *nous*, precisely the mind which is not involved in the soul, is immortal; and for Plato the immutability of ideas is regarded as a proof of the immortality of the spirit. (*b*) The dualism has the consequence for the doctrine of man of identifying the body with evil and of assuming the essential goodness of mind or spirit. This body-mind dualism and the value judgements passed upon both body and mind stand in sharpest contrast to the Biblical view of man, and achieve a fateful influence in all subsequent theories of human nature. The Bible knows nothing of a good mind and an evil body.

While Stoicism, as a monistic and pantheistic philosophy, sharply diverges from the Aristotelian and Platonic concepts in many respects, its view of human nature betrays more similarities than differences. The similarities are great enough, at any rate, to constitute it a part of the general 'classical' picture of man. The Stoic reason is more immanent in both the world process and in the soul and body of man than in Platonism; yet man is essentially reason. Even the dualism is not completely lacking. For while Stoicism is not always certain

[1] Cf. Werner Jaeger, *Aristotle*, Ch. VIII.

[2] Despite Aristotles naturalism, his psychology is dependent upon Plato's and it may be wrong to speak of his dualism as covert. It was fairly explicit. He believed that life without the body was the soul's normal state and that its sojourn in the body was a severe illness. Cf. Jaeger, ibid., p. 51.

whether the reason which governs man must persuade him
to emulate nature as he finds it outside of his reason or whether
it, being a special spark of the divine reason, must set him
against the impulses of nature, it arrives on the whole at con-
victions which do not qualify the classical concepts essentially.[1] The emphasis upon human freedom in its psychology
overcomes the pantheistic naturalism of its metaphysics; and
its completely negative attitude towards the passions and the
whole impulsive life of man sets reason in contrast to the
impulses of the body, however much it conceives reason as
basically the principle of harmony within the body.

Obviously, the Platonic, Aristotelian and Stoic conceptions
which define the 'classical' view of man do not exhaust Greek
speculations about human nature. Modern vitalism and
romanticism have their antecedents in the earlier Dionysian
religion, in Heraclitus'[2] conception of ultimate reality as Flux
and Fire and more particularly in the development of the
Dionysian theme in Greek tragedy.[3] Subsequent mysticism is
anticipated in Orphism and Pythagoreanism.[4] Even more significant for developments in contemporary culture, Democritus

[1] The confusion in Stoic thought between the reason in man and the
reason in nature, a confusion which was perpetuated constantly in
eighteenth-century borrowings from Stoicism, is clearly revealed in
Diogenes Laërtius' account of Zeno's thought. He writes: 'When
rational animals are endowed with reason in token of a more complete
superiority, life in them in accordance with nature is rightly understood
to mean life in accordance with reason. For reason is like a craftsman,
shaping impulses and desires. Hence Zeno's definition of the end is to
live in conformity with nature, which means to live a life of virtue; for
it is virtue to which nature leads. On the other hand a virtuous life is
one which conforms to our experience of the course of nature, our
human natures being parts of universal nature.' Diogenes Laërtius VII,
85.

[2] Heraclitus, *c.* 536–470 B.C., Greek philosopher. (Ed.)

[3] Nietzsche in his *Birth of Tragedy* claims the Greek dramatists too
unreservedly for his vitalistic philosophy. The significance of the
tragedies lies in the unresolved conflict between the Olympian and
Dionysian, the rational and the vitalistic, principles in Greek thought.
Significantly Zeus, the god of order and measure, remains the ultimate
arbiter in the Greek tragedies.

[4] Orphism: one of the Greek mystery-religions, flourishing in the
sixth century B.C. Pythagoreanism: the teaching of Pythagoras and his
school which were influential from the sixth to the fourth century B.C.
(Ed.)

and Epicurus[1] interpreted man, in accordance with their naturalism and materialism, not as standing outside of nature by the quality of his unique reason, but as wholly a part of nature. This Greek materialism was no less rationalistic than Platonism or Aristotelianism, but it reduced the immanental reason in the world to mechanical necessity and sought to understand man in terms of this mechanism. It was by combining Stoic with Democritan and Epicurean naturalism that modern culture arrived at concepts which were to express some of its most characteristic interpretations of man as primarily a child of nature.

It must be observed that, while the classical view of human virtue is optimistic when compared with the Christian view (for it finds no defect in the centre of human personality) and while it has perfect confidence in the virtue of the rational man, it does not share the confidence of the moderns in the ability of all men to be either virtuous or happy. Thus an air of melancholy hangs over Greek life which stands in sharpest contrast to the all-pervasive optimism of the now dying bourgeois culture, despite the assumption of the latter that it had merely restored the classical world view and the Greek view of man. 'There is nothing, methinks, more piteous than a man, of all things that creep and breathe upon the earth', declares Zeus in the *Iliad*, and that note runs as a consistent strain through Greek thought from Homer to the Hellenistic age. Primarily it was the brevity of life and the mortality of man which tempted the Greeks to melancholy. They were not dissuaded from this mood either by Plato's assurance of immortality nor yet by Epicurus' counsel that death need not be feared, since there was nothing on the other side of the grave.

Aristotle confessed that 'not to be born is the best thing and death is better than life', and gave it as his opinion that melancholy was a concomitant of genius. The philosophers were optimistic in their confidence that the wise man would be virtuous; but, alas, they had no confidence that the many could be wise. The Stoic Chrysippus[2] could conceive happiness

[1] Democritus (*c.* 460–360 B.C.), materialist philosopher. Epicurus (341–270 B.C.), taught that pleasure and happiness are the natural aims of life. (Ed.)

[2] Chrysippus (280–209 B.C.), one of the leaders of the Stoic School. (Ed.)

only for the wise and was certain that most men were fools. The Stoics tended on the one hand to include all men in the brotherhood of man on the ground that they all had the spark of divine reason; but on the other hand they pitied the multitude for having no obvious graces of rationality. Thus their equalitarianism rapidly degenerated into an aristocratic condescension not very different from Aristotle's contempt for the slave as a 'living tool'. Seneca,[1] despite his pious universalism, prays 'forgive the world: they are all fools'.

Neither Greek nor Roman classicists had any conception of a meaning in human history. History was a series of cycles, a realm of endless recurrences. Aristotle maintained that the arts and sciences were lost and found again not once but an infinite number of times.[2] Zeno envisaged the end of the world as a huge conflagration which would destroy the world's body. This pessimism about both man and his history is the natural consequence of the mind-body dualism which characterizes Greek thought far beyond the limits of Platonism. It culminated invariably in the conviction that the body is a tomb ($\sigma\tilde{\omega}\mu\alpha\sigma\tilde{\eta}\mu\alpha$),[3] a conviction which makes neo-Platonism the logical consummation of Greek thought.

The pessimism of Greek tragedy is somewhat different from that of the philosophers and most nearly approaches the Christian interpretation of life. But, unlike Christian thought, it has no answer for the problem it presents. In Aeschylus and Sophocles[4] the capricious jealousy of Zeus against mortal men of Homeric legend had been transmuted into the lawlessness of human passions. But, unlike the philosophers, the dramatists see human passions as something more than mere impulses of the body. The principle of order and measure, represented by Zeus, is constantly defied by vitalities in human life which are creative as well as destructive. The tragedy of human history consists precisely in the fact that human life cannot be creative without being destructive, that biological urges are enhanced

---

[1] Seneca (A.D. 4–65), a Roman stoic, and tutor of Nero. (Ed.)

[2] Cf. S. H. Butcher on 'The Melancholy of the Greeks', in *Some Aspects of the Greek Genius*.

[3] Cf. E. Bevan, *Stoics and Sceptics*, p. 100.

[4] Aeschylus (525–456 B.C.) and Sophocles (496–406 B.C.), Greek dramatists. (Ed.)

and sublimated by daemonic spirit and that this spirit cannot express itself without committing the sin of pride. The heroes of Greek tragedy are always being counselled to remember their mortality and to escape νέμεσις[1] by observing a proper restraint. But the ὕβρις which offends Zeus is an inevitable concomitant of their creative action in history. The tragic heroes are heroes precisely because they disregard this prudent advice of moderation. In that sense Greek tragedy is an explication of Nietzsche's observation: 'Every doer loves his deeds much more than it deserves to be loved; and the best deeds are born out of such an excess of love that they could not be worthy of it, even though their worth be very great.'[2] The various vitalities of human history are moreover not only in conflict with Zeus but in conflict with each other. There is no simple resolution of the conflict between the state and the family, usually symbolized as a conflict between man and woman, the latter representing the community of blood and family in contrast to the political community (as in *Iphigenia* at *Aulis* and in *Antigone*).[3] The conflict in Greek tragedy is, in short, between Gods, between Zeus and Dionysius; and not between God and the devil, nor between spirit and matter. The spirit of man expresses itself in his vital energies as well as in the harmonizing force of mind; and while the latter, as the rational principle of order, is the more ultimate (here the dramatists remain typically Greek) there can be creativity in human affairs only at the price of disturbing this order.

Thus life is at war with itself, according to Greek tragedy. There is no solution, or only a tragic solution, for the conflict between the vitalities of life and the principle of measure. Zeus remains God. But one is prompted to both admiration and pity toward those who defy him. It is significant that this profound problem posed by Greek tragedy was never sensed by the moderns, who revived classicism and ostensibly built their view of man upon Greek thought. They may have understood or misunderstood Plato and Aristotle; but the message of

[1] Retribution. (Ed.)

[2] *Kritik und Zukunft der Kultur*, Ch. IV, Par. 13.

[3] *Iphigenia at Aulis*, play by Euripides (480–406 B.C.); *Antigone*, play by Sophocles. (Ed.)

Aeschylus and Sophocles was neither understood nor mis-understood. It was simply neglected, except as the minor romantic note in modern culture appreciated and partly mis-understood it.

THE CHRISTIAN VIEW OF MAN

The Christian view of man, which modern culture ostensibly rejects in its entirety but by which its estimate of human nature is influenced more than it realizes, will be more fully analysed in this book. At this point we must briefly anticipate subse-quent elaborations by distinguishing the Christian view from the classical doctrine of man. As the classical view is deter-mined by Greek metaphysical presuppositions, so the Christian view is determined by the ultimate presuppositions of Christian faith. The Christian faith in God as Creator of the world trans-cends the canons and antinomies of rationality, particularly the antinomy between mind and matter, between consciousness and extension. God is not merely mind who forms a previously given formless stuff. God is both vitality and form and the source of all existence. He creates the world. This world is not God; but it is not evil because it is not God. Being God's creation, it is good.

The consequence of this conception of the world upon the view of human nature in Christian thought is to allow an appreciation of the unity of body and soul in human per-sonality which idealists and naturalists have sought in vain. Furthermore it prevents the idealistic error of regarding the mind as essentially good or essentially eternal and the body as essentially evil. But it also obviates the romantic error of seek-ing for the good in man-as-nature and for evil in man-as-spirit or as reason. Man is, according to the Biblical view, a created and finite existence in both body and spirit. Obviously a view which depends upon an ultra-rational presupposition is immediately endangered when rationally explicated; for reason, which seeks to bring all things into terms of rational coherence, is tempted to make one known thing the principle of explanation and to derive all other things from it. Its most natural inclination is to make itself that ultimate principle, and thus in effect to declare itself God. Christian psychology and philosophy have never completely freed themselves from this fault, which explains why naturalists plausibly though erroneously regard Christian faith as the very fountain source of idealism.

This is also the reason why the Biblical view of the unity of man as body and soul has often seemed to be no more than the consequence of primitive Hebraic psychology. In Hebrew thought the soul of man resides in his blood and the concept of an immortal mind in a mortal body remains unknown to the end. It is true that certain distinctions are gradually made. At first both *ruach* and *nephesh*[1] mean little more than 'breath'; but they are gradually distinguished and *ruach* becomes roughly synonymous with spirit or *nous* and *nephesh* with soul or *psyche*. But, unlike Greek thought, this distinction does not lead to dualistic consequences. The monism of the Biblical view is something other than the failure to differentiate *physis, psyche* and *nous*, which characterized Greek thought before Anaxagoras[2]; nor is it merely the consequence of an undeveloped psychology. It is ultimately derived from the Biblical view of God as the Creator of the Biblical faith in the goodness of creation.

The second important characteristic of the Christian view of man is that he is understood primarily from the standpoint of God, rather than from the uniqueness of his rational faculties or his relation to nature. He is made in the 'image of God'. It has been the mistake of many Christian rationalists to assume that this term is no more than a religious-pictorial expression of what philosophy intends when it defines man as a rational animal. We have previously alluded to the fact that the human spirit has the special capacity of standing continually outside itself in terms of indefinite regression. Consciousness is a capacity for surveying the world and determining action from a governing centre. Self-consciousness represents a further degree of transcendence in which the self makes itself its own object

---

[1] *ruach*, Hebrew for 'breath, wind, the Spirit'; *nephesh*, Hebrew for 'self'. (Ed.)

[2] Anaxagoras (*c.* 430 B.C.), Greek philosopher. (Ed.)

in such a way that the ego is finally always subject and not object. The rational capacity of surveying the world, of forming general concepts and analysing the order of the world, is thus but one aspect of what Christianity knows as 'spirit'. The self knows the world, in so far as it knows the world, because it stands outside both itself and the world, which means that it cannot understand itself except as it is understood from beyond itself and the world.

This essential homelessness of the human spirit is the ground of all religion; for the self which stands outside itself and the world cannot find the meaning of life in itself or the world. It cannot identify meaning with causality in nature; for its freedom is obviously something different from the necessary causal links of nature. Nor can it identify the principle of meaning with rationality, since it transcends its own rational processes, so that it may, for instance, ask the question whether there is a relevance between its rational forms and the recurrences and forms of nature. It is this capacity of freedom which finally prompts great cultures and philosophies to transcend rationalism, and to seek for the meaning of life in an unconditioned ground of existence. But from the standpoint of human thought this unconditioned ground of existence, this God, can be defined only negatively. This is why mystic religions in general, and particularly the neo-Platonic tradition in Western culture, have one interesting similarity with Christianity and one important difference in their estimate of human nature. In common with Christianity they measure the depth of the human spirit in terms of its capacity for self-transcendence. Thus Plotinus defines *nous* not as Aristotle defines it. For him it is primarily the capacity for self-knowledge and it has no limit short of the eternal. Mysticism and Christianity agree in understanding man from the standpoint of the eternal. But since mysticism leads to an undifferentiated ultimate reality, it is bound to regard particularity, including individuality, as essentially evil. All mystic religions therefore have the characteristic of accentuating individuality, in as far as individuality is inherent in the capacity for self-consciousness emphasized in mysticism and is something more than mere bodily particularity; but all mystic philosophies ultimately lose the very individuality which they first emphasize, because they sink finite particularity in a distinctionless divine ground of existence.

God as will and personality, in concepts of Christian faith, is thus the only possible ground of real individuality, though not the only possible presupposition of self-consciousness. But faith in God as will and personality depends upon faith in His power to reveal Himself. The Christian faith in God's self-disclosure culminating in the revelation of Christ, is thus the basis of the Christian concept of personality and individuality. In terms of this faith man can understand himself as a unity of will which finds its end in the will of God. We thus have in the problem of human nature one of the many indications of the relation of general and special revelation which concerns theology so perennially. The conviction that man stands too completely outside of both nature and reason to understand himself in terms of either without misunderstanding himself, belongs to general revelation in the sense that any astute analysis of the human situation must lead to it. But if man lacks a further revelation of the divine he will also misunderstand himself when he seeks to escape the conditions of nature and reason. He will end by seeking absorption in a divine reality which is at once all and nothing. To understand himself truly means to begin with a faith that he is understood from beyond himself, that he is known and loved of God and must find himself in terms of obedience to the divine will. This relation of the divine to the human will makes it possible for man to relate himself to God without pretending to be God, and to accept his distance from God as a created thing without believing that the evil of his nature is caused by this finiteness. Man's finite existence in the body and in history can be essentially affirmed, as naturalism wants to affirm it. Yet the uniqueness of man's spirit can be appreciated even more than idealism appreciates it, though always preserving a proper distinction between the human and divine. Also the unity of spirit and body can be emphasized in terms of its relation to a Creator and Redeemer who created both mind and body. These are the ultra-rational foundations and presuppositions of Christian wisdom about man.

This conception of man's stature is not, however, the complete Christian picture of man. The high estimate of the human stature implied in the concept of 'image of God' stands in paradoxical juxtaposition to the low estimate of human virtue in Christian thought. Man is a sinner. His sin is defined as rebellion against God. The Christian estimate of human evil is so serious precisely because it places evil at the very centre of human personality—in the will. This evil cannot be regarded complacently as the inevitable consequence of his finiteness or the fruit of his involvement in the contingencies and necessities of nature. Sin is occasioned precisely by the fact that man refuses to admit his 'creatureliness' and to acknowledge himself as merely a member of a total unity of life. He pretends to be more than he is. Nor can he, as in both rationalistic and mystic dualism, dismiss his sins as residing in that part of himself which is not his true self, that is, that part of himself which is involved in physical necessity. In Christianity it is not the eternal man who judges the finite man; but the eternal and holy God who judges sinful man. Nor is redemption in the power of the eternal man who gradually sloughs off finite man. Man is not divided against himself so that the essential man can be extricated from the non-essential. Man contradicts himself within the terms of his true essence. His essence is free self-determination. His sin is the wrong use of his freedom and its consequent destruction.

Man is an individual, but he is not self-sufficing. The law of his nature is love, a harmonious relation of life to life in obedience to the divine centre and source of his life. This law is violated when man seeks to make himself the centre and source of his own life. His sin is therefore spiritual and not carnal, though the infection of rebellion spreads from the spirit to the body and disturbs its harmonies also. Man, in other words, is a sinner not because he is one limited individual within a whole but rather because he is betrayed, by his very ability to survey the whole, to imagine himself the whole.

The fact that human vitality inevitably expresses itself in defiance of the laws of measure can be observed without the presuppositions of the Christian faith. The analysis of this fact in Greek tragedy has already been observed. But it is impossible without the presuppositions of the Christian faith to find the source of sin within man himself. Greek tragedy regards human evil as the consequence of a conflict between vitality and form, between Dionysian and Olympian divinities. Only in a religion of revelation, whose God reveals Himself to man from beyond himself and from beyond the contrast of vitality and form, can man discover the root of sin to be within himself. The essence of man is his freedom. Sin is committed in that freedom. Sin can therefore not be attributed to a defect in his essence. It can only be understood as a self-contradiction, made possible by the fact of his freedom but not following necessarily from it.

Christianity, therefore, issues inevitably in the religious expression of an uneasy conscience. Only within terms of the Christian faith can man not only understand the reality of the evil in himself, but escape the error of attributing that evil to any one but himself. It is possible of course to point out that man is tempted by the situation in which he stands. He stands at the juncture of nature and spirit. The freedom of his spirit causes him to break the harmonies of nature, and the pride of his spirit prevents him from establishing a new harmony. The freedom of his spirit enables him to use the forces and processes of nature creatively; but his failure to observe the limits of his finite existence causes him to defy the forms and restraints of both nature and reason. Human self-consciousness is a high tower looking upon a large and inclusive world. It vainly imagines that it is the large world which it beholds and not a narrow tower insecurely erected amidst the shifting sands of the world.

(FROM: *The Nature and Destiny of Man*, Vol. I, pp. 1–18.)

2 'WHERE A CHRIST IS, AND IS NOT, EXPECTED'

[In this section Niebuhr provides a useful key for classifying and studying the religions of the world. Religions 'where a Christ is expected' are those which take history and time seriously since it is believed that they are vehicles of divine revelation. Judaism and Christianity are examples of such religions. Religions 'where a Christ is not expected' are those where history and time are not taken seriously because they belong to the world of unreality, what the Hindus call *maya* (illusion). Examples of such religions would be Graeco-Roman religion, Hinduism and Buddhism.]

A basic distinction may be made between various interpretations of the meaning of life by noting their attitude towards history. Those which include history in the realm of meaning see it as a process which points and moves towards a fuller disclosure and realization of life's essential meaning. Those which exclude it, do so because they regard history as no more than natural finiteness, from which the human spirit must be freed. They consider man's involvement in nature as the very cause of evil, and define the ultimate redemption of life as emancipation from finiteness. In the one case history is regarded as potentially meaningful, waiting for the ultimate disclosure and realization of its meaning. In the other case it is believed to be essentially meaningless. It may be regarded as a realm of order; but the order is only the subordinate one of natural necessity which affects the meaning of life negatively. It is a mortal coin which must be shuffled off.

The difference in the attitude of various cultures towards history is determined by contradictory estimates of man's transcendence over himself. In the one case it is assumed that since this capacity for self-transcendence represents the highest capacity of the human spirit, the fulfilment of life must naturally consist in man's emancipation from the ambiguities of history. His partial immersion in and partial transcendence over nature must be transmuted into a total transcendence. Some sort of eternity is therefore the goal of human striving in non-historical religions and philosophies; and the eternity which is man's end is the fulfilment of history to the point of being its negation. In this eternity there is 'no separation of thing from thing, no part standing in isolated existence estranged from the rest and therefore nowhere is there any wronging of another'.[1]

In religions which regard history as contributing to the meaning of life the attitude towards man's partial involvement in, and partial transcendence over, the process of nature and

[1] Plotinus, *Enneads*, III, ii:1.

the flux of time is totally different. This ambiguous situation is not regarded as the evil from which man must be redeemed. The evil in the human situation arises, rather, from the fact that men seek to deny or to escape prematurely from the uncertainties of history and to claim a freedom, a transcendence and an eternal and universal perspective which is not possible for finite creatures. The problem of sin rather than finiteness is, in other words, either implicitly or explicitly the basic problem of life. Yet the problem of finiteness is not eliminated. It is recognized that a man who stands in an historical process is too limited in vision to discern the full meaning of that process, and too limited in power to fulfil the meaning, however much the freedom of his knowledge and his power is one element in the stuff of history. Hence the temporal problem of human history and destiny in historical religion is: how the transcendent meaning of history is to be disclosed and fulfilled, since man can discern only partial meanings and can only partially realize the meaning he discerns. In modern corruptions of historical religion this problem is solved very simply by the belief that the cumulative effects of history will endow weak man with both the wisdom and the power to discern and to fulfil life's meaning.

In the more profound versions of historical religion it is recognized, however, that there is no point in history, whatever the cumulations of wisdom and power, in which the finiteness of man is overcome so that he could complete his own life, or in which history as such does not retain the ambiguity of being rooted in nature-necessity on the one hand while pointing towards transcendent, 'eternal' and trans-historical ends on the other hand.

Historical religions are therefore by their very nature prophetic-Messianic. They look forward at first to a point in history and finally towards an eschaton (end) which is also the end of history, where the full meaning of life and history will be disclosed and fulfilled. Significantly, as in the optimistic expectations of a 'day of the Lord' which the first great literary prophet, Amos, found at hand and criticized, these Messianic expectations begin as expressions of national hope and expectations of national triumph. Only gradually it is realized that man's effort to deny and to escape his finiteness in imperial ambitions and power add an element of corruption to the fabric of history and that this corruption becomes a basic characteristic of history and a perennial problem from the standpoint of the fulfilment of human history and destiny. It is recognized that history must be purged as well as completed; and that the final completion of history must include God's destruction of man's abortive and premature efforts to bring history to its culmination.

The basic distinction between historical and non-historical religions and cultures may thus be succinctly defined as the difference between those which expect and those which do not expect a Christ. A Christ is expected wherever history is regarded as potentially meaningful but as still awaiting the full disclosure and fulfilment of its meaning. A Christ is not expected wherever the meaning of life is explained from the standpoint of either nature or supernature in such a way that a transcendent revelation of history's meaning is not regarded as either possible or necessary. It is not regarded as possible when, as in various forms of naturalism, the visions and ambitions of historical existence which point beyond nature are regarded as illusory, and nature-history is believed to be incapable of receiving disclosures of meaning which point beyond itself. It is not regarded as necessary when man's capacity for freedom and self-transcendence is believed to be infinitely extensible until the ambiguities of history are left behind and pure eternity is achieved. The significance of a Christ is that he is a disclosure of the divine purpose, governing history within history. Wherever it is believed that man's capacity to transcend self and history can be dissociated from his finiteness, the meaning of salvation is conceived as essentially redemption from history, obviating any necessity of, or desire for, the fulfilment of man in history, or for the disclosure of history's ultimate meaning.

A Christ is expected wherever history is thought of as a realm of fragmentary revelations of a purpose and power transcending history, pointing to a fuller disclosure of that purpose and power. He is expected because this disclosure is regarded as both possible and necessary. It is regarded as possible because history is known to be something more than the nature-necessity in which it has its roots. It is regarded as necessary because the potential meaningfulness of history is recognized as fragmentary and corrupted. It must be completed and clarified.

The interpretation of the cultures of the world in this fashion according to their possession, or lack, of Messianic expectations, draws upon insights which are possible only after the logic of Messianic expectations has reached its culmination in the Christian belief that these expectations have been fulfilled in Christ. It is not possible to interpret cultures according to their expectation or want of expectation of *a* Christ without drawing upon the faith that *the* Christ has been revealed; for there can be no interpretation of the meaning of life and history without implicitly or explicitly drawing into the interpretation the faith which claims to have found the end of these expectations. This is to say, merely, that there can be no interpretation of history without specific presuppositions and that the interpretation which is being attempted in these pages is based upon Christian presuppositions. The Christian answer to the problem of life is assumed in the discussion of the problem. In that sense our interpretation is, as every interpretation must be in the final analysis, 'dogmatic' or confessional. Yet it is not purely dogmatic or confessional; for it seeks to analyse the question and expectations for which a particular epic of history is regarded as the answer, and also to determine why these questions and expectations are not universal in history. Such an analysis must begin with a further inquiry into the character of non-historical forms of culture which regard Christ as 'foolishness' because they have no questions for which Christ is the answer and no expectations and hopes for which his Cross is the fulfilment.

(FROM: *The Nature and Destiny of Man*, Vol. II, pp. 2–6.)

3   ON MYTH AND ITS PLACE IN THE CHRISTIAN RELIGION

[In this extract from one of what Niebuhr called his 'sermonic essays' he provides a powerful argument for the necessity of myth and metaphor in religious, and especially Christian language. In the course of the argument he discusses in an illuminating way the permanent truth and value of the 'myths' of Creation, 'The Fall of Man', Incarnation and Atonement, Judgement to come. Readers will find it instructive to compare this extract with those by Bultmann and Tillich on 'myth' (see Vol. 2, pp. 64ff and Vol. 3, pp. 47ff).]

Among the paradoxes with which St Paul describes the character, the vicissitudes and the faith of the Christian ministry, the phrase 'as deceivers yet true' is particularly intriguing. Following immediately after the phrase 'by evil report and good report' it probably defines the evil reports which were circulated about him as charges of deception and dishonesty. This charge is refuted with his 'yet true'. But the question arises why the charge is admitted before it is refuted. Perhaps this is done merely for the sake of preserving an unbroken line of paradoxical statements. If this be the case, a mere canon of rhetorical style has prompted a very profound statement. For what is true in the Christian religion can be expressed only in symbols which contain a certain degree of provisional and superficial deception. Every apologist of the Christian faith might well, therefore, make the Pauline phrase his own. We do teach the truth by deception. We are deceivers, yet true.

The necessity for the deception is given in the primary characteristic of the Christian world view. Christianity does not believe that the natural, temporal and historic world is self-derived or self-explanatory. It believes that the ground and the fulfilment of existence lie outside of existence, in an eternal and divine will. But it does not hold, as do many forms of dualism, that there is an eternal world separate and distinct from the temporal world. The relation between the temporal and the eternal is dialectical. The eternal is revealed and expressed in the temporal but not exhausted in it. God is not the sum total of finite occasions and relationships. He is their ground and they are the creation of His will. But, on the other hand, the finite world is not merely a corrupt emanation from the ideal and eternal. Consequently the relation of time and eternity cannot be expressed in simple rational terms. It can be expressed only in symbolic terms. A rational or logical expression of the relationship invariably leads either to a pantheism in which God and the world are identified, and the temporal in its totality is equated with the eternal; or in which they are separated so that a false super-naturalism emerges, a dualism between an eternal and spiritual world without content and a temporal world without meaning or significance.

I

Before analysing the deceptive symbols which the Christian faith uses to express this dimension of eternity in time, it might be clarifying to recall that artists are forced to use deceptive symbols when they seek to portray two dimensions of space upon the single dimension of a flat canvas. Every picture which suggests depth and perspective draws angles not as they are but as they appear to the eye when it looks into depth. Parallel lines are not drawn as parallel lines but are made to appear as if they converged on the horizon; for so they appear to the eye when it envisages a total perspective. Only the most primitive art and the drawings made by very small children reveal the mistake of portraying things in their true proportions rather than as they are seen. The necessity of picturing things as they seem rather than as they are, in order to record on one dimension what they are in two dimensions, is a striking analogy, in the field of space, of the problem of religion in the sphere of time.

Time is a succession of events. Yet mere succession is not time. Time has reality only through a meaningful relationship of its successions. Therefore time is real only as it gives successive expressions of principles and powers which lies outside of it. Yet every suggestion of the principle of a process must be expressed in terms of the temporal process, and every idea of the God who is the ground of the world must be expressed in some term taken from the world. The temporal process is like the painter's flat canvas. It is one dimension upon which two dimensions must be recorded. This can be done only by symbols which deceive for the sake of truth.

Great art faces the problem of the two dimensions of time as well as the two dimensions of space. The portrait artist, for instance, is confronted with the necessity of picturing a character. Human personality is more than succession of moods. The moods of a moment are held together in a unity of thought and feeling, which gives them, however seemingly capricious, a considerable degree of consistency. The problem of the artist is to portray the inner consistency of a character which is never fully expressed in any one particular mood or facial expression. This can be done only by falsifying physiognomic details. Portraiture is an art which can never be sharply distinguished from caricature. A moment of time in a personality can be made to express what transcends the moment of time only if the moment is not recorded accurately. It must be made into a symbol of something beyond itself.

This technique of art explains why art is more closely related to religion than science. Art describes the world not in terms of its exact relationships. It constantly falsifies these relationships, as analysed by science, in order to express their total meaning.

II

The Christian religion may be characterized as one which has transmuted primitive religious and artistic myths and symbols without fully rationalizing them. Buddhism is much more rational than Christianity. In consequence Buddhism finds the finite and temporal world evil. Spinozism is a more rational version of God and the world than the biblical account; but it finds the world unqualifiedly good and identical with God. In the biblical account the world is good because God created it; but the world is not God. Every Christian myth, in one way or another, expresses both the meaningfulness and the incompleteness of the temporal world, both the majesty of God and his relation to the world.

We are deceivers yet true, when we say that God created the world. Creation is a mythical idea which cannot be fully rationalized. It has therefore been an offence to the philosophers who, with the scientists, have substituted the idea of causality for it. They have sought to explain each subsequent event by a previous cause. Such an explanation of the world leads the more naïve thinkers to a naturalism which regards the world as self-explanatory because every event can be derived from a previous one. The more sophisticated philosophers will at least, with Aristotle, seek for a first cause which gives an original impetus to the whole chain of causation. But such a first cause does not have a living relationship with the events of nature and history. It does not therefore account for the emergence of novelty in each new event. No new fact or event in history is an arbitrary novelty. It is always related to a previous event. But it is a great error to imagine that this relationship completely accounts for the new emergence. In both nature and history each new thing is only one of an infinite number of possibilities which might have emerged at that particular juncture. It is for this reason that, though we can trace a series of causes in retrospect, we can never predict the future with accuracy. There is a profound arbitrariness in every given fact, which rational theories of causation seek to obscure. Thus they regard a given form of animal life as rational because they can trace it historically to another form or relate it in terms of genus and species to other types of life. Yet none of these relationships, whether historical or schematic, can eliminate the profound arbitrariness of the givenness of things.

It is therefore true, to account for the meaningfulness of life in terms of the relation of every thing to a creative centre and source of meaning. But the truth of creation can be expressed only in terms which outrage reason. Involved in the idea of creation is the concept of making something out of nothing. The *Shepherd* of Hermas[1] declares 'First of all believe that God is one, who created and set in order all things and caused the universe to exist out of nothing.' This was the constant reiteration of Christian belief, until in very modern times it was thought possible to substitute the idea of evolutionary

[1] A second-century Christian writing. (Ed.)

causation for the idea of creation. The idea of creation out of nothing is profoundly ultrarational; for human reason can deal only with the stuff of experience, and in experience the previous event and cause are seen, while the creative source of novelty is beyond experience.

The idea of creation relates the ground of existence to existence and is therefore mythical rather than rational. The fact that it is not a rational idea does not make it untrue or deceptive. But since it is not rational it is a temptation to deceptions. Every mythical idea contains a primitive deception and a more ultimate one. The primitive error is to regard the early form in which the myth is stated as authoritative. Thus the Christian religion is always tempted to insist that belief in creation also involves belief in an actual forming of man out of a lump of clay, or in an actual creative activity of six days. It is to this temptation that biblical literalism succumbs. But there is also a more ultimate source of error in the mythical statement of religious belief. That is to regard the relation of each fact and event in history to a Divine Creator as obviating the possibility of an organic relation to other facts and events according to a natural order. By this error, which Etienne Gilson[1] calls 'theologism,' Christian theology is constantly tempted to deny the significance of the natural order, and to confuse the scientific analysis of its relationships. At the rise of modern thought Malebranche developed a doctrine of 'occasionalism' which expressed this error of Christian theology in its most consistent form. But it has been a persistent error in Christian thought and one which arises naturally out of the mythical statement of the idea of creation. The error is analogous to that of certain types of art which completely falsify the natural relations of objects in order to express their ultimate significance.

We are deceivers, yet true, when we say that men fell into evil. The story of the fall of man in the Garden of Eden is a primitive myth which modern theology has been glad to disavow, for fear that modern culture might regard belief in it as a proof of the obscurantism of religion. In place of it we have substituted various accounts of the origin and the nature of evil in human life. Most of these accounts, reduced to their

[1] In his *Unity of Philosophical Experience.*

essentials, attribute sin to the inertia of nature, or the hypertrophy of impulses, or to the defect of reason (ignorance), and thereby either explicitly or implicitly place their trust in developed reason as the guarantor of goodness. In all of these accounts the essential point in the nature of human evil is missed, namely that it arises from the very freedom of reason with which man is endowed. Sin is not so much a consequence of natural impulses, which in animal life do not lead to sin, as of the freedom by which man is able to throw the harmonies of nature out of joint. He disturbs the harmony of nature when he centres his life about one particular impulse (sex or the possessive impulse, for instance) or when he tries to make himself, rather than God, the centre of existence. This egoism is sin in its quintessential form. It is not a defect of creation but a defect which becomes possible because man has been endowed with a freedom not known in the rest of creation.

The idea of the fall is subject to the error of regarding the primitive myth of the garden, the apple and the serpent, as historically true. But even if this error is not committed, Christian thought is still tempted to regard the fall as an historical occurrence. The fall is not historical. It does not take place in any concrete human act. It is the presupposition of such acts. It deals with an area of human freedom which, when once expressed in terms of an act, is always historically related to a previous act or predisposition. External descriptions of human behaviour are therefore always deterministic. That is the deception into which those are betrayed who seek to avoid the errors of introspection by purely external descriptions of human behaviour. What Christianity means by the idea of the fall can only be known in introspection. The consciousness of sin and the consciousness of God are inextricably involved with each other. Only as the full dimension of human existence is measured, which includes not only the dimension of historical breadth but the dimension of transhistorical freedom, does the idea of the fall of man achieve significance.

It is interesting to note that Christian theology has usually regarded the fall as an historical occurrence, even when it did not accept the primitive myth of the Garden of Eden. It therefore spoke of a perfection before the fall as if that too were an historical era. Even the sophisticated dialectical theology of Barth and his school speaks of the perfection before the fall as historical, and consequently elaborates a doctrine of human sinfulness which approaches, and sometimes surpasses, the extremism of the historic doctrine of total depravity. The perfection before the fall is an ideal possibility which men can comprehend but not realize. The perfection before the fall is, in a sense, the perfection before the act. Thus we are able to conceive of a perfectly disinterested justice; but when we act our own achievements will fall short of this standard. The rationalists always assume that, since men are able to conceive of perfect standards of justice, such standards will be realized as soon as all men become intelligent enough to conceive them. They do not realize that intelligence offers no guarantee of the realization of a standard, and that the greatest idealists, as well as the most cynical realists or the most ignorant victims of an immediate situation, fall short in their action; nor that such falling short arises not simply from the defect of the mind but from an egoistic corruption of the heart. Self intrudes itself into every ideal, when thought gives place to action. The deceptions to which the idea of the fall give rise are many; and all of them have been the basis of error at some time or other in the history of Christian theology. We are deceivers, yet true in clinging to the idea of the fall as a symbol of the origin and the nature of evil in human life.

III

We are deceivers, yet true, when we affirm that God became man to redeem the world from sin. The idea of eternity entering time is intellectually absurd. This absurdity is proved to the hilt by all the theological dogmas which seek to make it rational. The dogmas which seek to describe the relation of God the Father (the God who does not enter history) and God the son (the God of history) all insist that the Son is equal to the Father and yet is not equal to Him. In the same way all the doctrines of the two natures of Christ assert that he is not less divine for being human and temporal and not less human and temporal for being fully divine. Quite obviously it is impossible to assert that the eternal ground of existence has entered existence and not sacrificed its eternal and unconditioned quality, without outraging every canon of reason. Reason may deal with the conditioned realities of existence in their relationships and it may even point to the fathomless depth of creativity out of which existential forms are born. But it cannot assert that the Divine Creator has come into creation without losing His unconditioned character. The truth that the Word was made flesh outrages all the canons by which truth is usually judged. Yet it is the truth. The whole character of the Christian religion is involved in that affirmation. It asserts that God's word is relevant to human life. It declares that an event in history can be of such a character as to reveal the character of history itself; that without such a revelation the character of history cannot be known. It is not possible to arrive at an understanding of the meaning of life and history without such a revelation. No induction from empirical facts can yield a conclusion about ultimate meaning because every process of induction presupposes some canon and criterion of meaning. That is why metaphysical systems which pretend to arrive at ultimate conclusions about the meaning of life are either covert theologies which unconsciously rationalize some revelation, accepted by faith; or they merely identify rationality with meaning, a procedure which forces them into either pantheism or acosmism. They must either identify the world with God on the supposition that temporal events, fully understood in all their relationships, are transmuted from finiteness and contingency into an unconditioned totality; or they must find the existential world evil in its finiteness because it does not conform in its contingent, existential relationships to a rational idea of unity.

For Christian faith the world is neither perfect nor meaningless. The God who created it also reveals Himself in it. He reveals Himself not only in a general revelation, that is, in the sense that His creation is His revelation; but in a special revelation. A general revelation can only point to the reality of God but not to His particular attributes. A theology which believes only in a general revelation must inevitably culminate in pantheism; because a God who is merely the object of human knowledge and not a subject who communicates with man by His own initiative is something less than God. A knowledge of God which depends only upon a study of the behaviour of the world must inevitably be as flat as the knowledge of any person would be, which depended merely upon the observation of the person's behaviour. The study of human behaviour cannot give a full clue to the meaning of a personality, because there is a depth of freedom in every personality which can only communicate itself in its own 'word.' That word may be related to an analysis. But it is not the consequence of the analysis. Without such a word the picture of any personality would be flat, as the interpretations of the divine which eliminate revelation are flat.

In Christian thought Christ is both the perfect man, 'the second Adam' who had restored the perfection of what man was and ought to be; and the Son of God, who transcends all possibilties of human life. It is this idea which theology sought to rationalize and yet it is a true idea. Human life stands in infinity. Everything it touches turns into infinity. Every moral standard, rigorously analysed, proves to be no permanently valid standard at all short of perfect and infinite love. The only adequate norm of human conduct is love of God and of man, through which all men are perfectly related to each other, because they are all related in terms of perfect obedience and love to the centre and source of their existence. In the same way all evil in human life is derived from an effort to transmute finite values into infinities, to seek infinite power, and infinite wealth and infinite gratification of desire. There is no sharp line between infinity in man and the infinity beyond man and yet there is a very sharp line. Man always remains a creature and his sin arises from the fact that he is not satisfied to remain so. He seeks to turn creatureliness into infinity; whereas his salvation depends upon subjecting his creaturely weakness to the infinite good of God. Christ, who expresses both the infinite possibilities beyond human life, is thus a true revelation of the total situation in which human life stands. There is every possibility of illusion and deception in this statement of the Christian faith. Men may be deceived by the primitive myth of the Virgin Birth and seek to comprehend as a pure historical fact, what is significant precisely because it points beyond history. Or they may seek to explain the dogma of the Incarnation in terms which will make it an article in a philosophical creed. Such efforts will lead to varied deceptions; but the deceptions cannot destroy the truth of the Incarnation.

Yet the revelation of God in the Incarnation is not of itself the redemption. Christianity believes that Christ died to save men from sin. It has a gospel which contains a crucifixion as well as an incarnation, a cross as well as a manger. This doctrine of the atoning death of the Son of God upon the cross has led to many theological errors, among them to theories of substitutionary atonement which outrage the moral sense. There is in fact no theory of the atonement which is quite as satisfying as the simple statements of the vicarious death of Christ in the Gospels. This may mean that faith is able to sense and appropriate an ultimate truth too deep for human reason. This is the foolishness of God which is wiser than the wisdom of men. The modern world has found not only the theories of atonement but the idea of atonement itself absurd. It rebelled not only against theories of a sacrifice which ransomed man from the devil's clutches or of a sacrifice which appeased the anger of a vindictive divine Father; it regarded the very idea of reconciliation between God and man as absurd.

The reason for this simple rejection of the Christian drama of salvation lies in the modern conception of human nature, rather than in any rejection of the theological absurdities attached to the idea of Christ's atoning death. Modern man does not regard life as tragic. He thinks that history is the record of the progressive triumph of good over evil. He does not recognize the simple but profound truth that man's life remains self-contradictory in its sin, no matter how high human culture rises; that the highest expression of human spirituality, therefore, contains also the subtlest form of human sin. The failure to recognize this fact gives modern culture a non-tragic conception of human history. To recognize this fact, and nothing more, is to reduce human history to simple tragedy. But the basic message of Christian faith is a message of hope in tragedy. It declares that when the Christ, by whom the world was made, enters the world, the world will not receive him. 'He came unto his own and his own received him not.' Human existence denies its own deepest and most essential nature. That is tragic. But when that fact is understood, when men cease to make the standards of a sinful existence the norms of life but accept its true norm, even though they fail to obey it, their very contrition opens the eyes of faith. This is the Godly sorrow that worketh repentence. Out of this despair hope is born. The hope is simply this: that the contradictions of human existence, which man cannot surmount, are swallowed up in the life of God Himself. The God of Christian faith is not only creator but redeemer. He does not allow human existence to end tragically. He snatches victory from defeat. He is Himself defeated in history but He is also victorious in that defeat.

There are theologies which interpret this article in the Christian creed as if life were really pure tragedy, but for the atoning love of Christ. But the fact is that the atoning death of Christ is the revelation of ultimate reality which may become the principle of interpretation for all human experience. It is not a principle yielded by experience, but it is applicable to experience and validated by it. It is an actual fact that human life, which is always threatened and periodically engulfed by the evil which human sin creates, is also marvellously redeemed by the transmutation of evil into good. This transmutation is not a human but a divine possibility. No man can, by taking thought, turn evil into good. Yet in the total operations of providence in history this transmutation occurs. The Christian faith consequently does not defy the tragic facts of human existence by a single victory over tragedy; nor does it flee the tragedy of temporal existence into a heavenly escape. These forms of the Christian faith are deceptions.

Most profoundly the atonement of Christ is a revelation of what life actually is. It is tragic from the standpoint of human striving. Human striving can do no better than the Roman law and the Hebraic religion, both the highest of their kind, through which the Lord was crucified. Yet this crucifixion becomes the revelation of that in human history which transcends human striving. And without this revelation, that which is beyond tragedy in life could not have been apprehended.

Without the cross men are beguiled by what is good in human existence into a false optimism and by what is tragic into despair. The message of the Son of God who dies upon the cross, of a God who transcends history and is yet in history, who condemns and judges sin and yet suffers with and for the sinner, this message is the truth about life. It cannot be stated without deceptions; but the truths which seek to avoid the deceptions are immeasurably less profound. Compared to this Christ who died for men's sins upon the cross, Jesus, the good man who tells all men to be good, is more solidly historical. But he is the bearer of no more than a pale truism.

We are deceivers, yet true, when we declare that Christ will come again at the last judgement, that he who was defeated in history will ultimately triumph over it, will become its judge and the author of its new life. No doctrine of Christianity has led to more deceptions and illusions than the hope of the second coming of Christ. This doctrine has been so frequently appropriated and exploited by sectarian fanatics that the Church has been a little ashamed of it. We have made even less of the apocalyptic literature into which Hebraic prophecy culminated and in which Christ was nurtured. The imagery of this literature is so extravagant, and at times so fantastic, that Christian thinkers have been content, on the whole, to leave it alone. Yet the doctrine of Christ's second coming involves all the profoundest characteristics of the Christian religion. It is this doctrine which distinguishes Christianity both from naturalistic utopianism and from Hellenistic otherworldliness. In it the Christian hope of the fulfilment of life is expressed paradoxically and dialectically, holding fast to its essential conception of the relation of time to eternity. History is not regarded as meaningless, as in Greek thought, particularly in later neo-Platonism. For this reason the realm of fulfilment is not above history, in some heaven in which pure form is abstracted from the concrete content of historical existence. The realm of fulfilment is at the end of history. This symbolizes that fulfilment both transcends and is relevant to historical forms. The end of history is not a point in history.

The chronological illusion, that it is a point in history, so characteristic of all myths which point to the trans-historical by a symbol of time, is particularly fruitful of error in the doctrine of the second coming. It has led to fantastic sectarian illusions of every type. Yet it is significant that the dispossessed and disinherited have been particularly prone to these illusions, because they were anxious to express the Christian hope of fulfilment in social as well as in individual terms. Sectarian apocalypticism is closely related to modern proletarian radicalism, which is a secularized form of the latter. In both, the individualism of Christian orthodoxy is opposed with conceptions which place the corporate enterprises of mankind, as well as individuals, under an ultimate judgement and under ultimate possibilities of fulfilment. In these secular and apocalyptic illusions the end of time is a point in time beyond which there will be an unconditioned society. But there is truth in the illusions.

The more bourgeois version of this illusory apocalypticism is the idea of progress in which the unconditioned ground of history is explicitly denied, but an unconditioned fulfilment in terms of infinite duration is implicitly affirmed. The Kingdom of God, as the absolute reign of God, is transmuted into a principle of development, immanent in history itself. Against such a conception Christian thought is forced to maintain as rigorous opposition as against dualistic otherworldliness. The ultimate fulfilment of life transcends the possibilities of human history. There is no hope of overcoming the contradictions, in which life stands, in history. But since these contradictions are not the consequence of mere finiteness and temporality, but the fruits of human freedom, they are not overcome merely by translating the temporal into the eternal. Since they persist in all human striving, fulfilment is not a human but a divine possibility. God must overcome this inescapable contradiction.

Therefore it is Christ who is both the judge of the world and the author of its fulfilment; for Christ is the symbol both of what man ought to be and of what God is beyond man. In Christ we have a revelation of both the human possibilities which are to be fulfilled and the divine power which will fulfil them. In Christ, too, we have the revelation of the significance of human history and of the ground of its meaning which transcends history.

We are therefore deceivers, yet true, when we insist that the

Christ who died on the cross will come again in power and glory, that he will judge the quick and the dead and will establish his Kingdom. We do not believe that the human enterprise will have a tragic conclusion; but the ground of our hope lies not in human capacity but in divine power and mercy, in the character of the ultimate reality, which carries the human enterprise. This hope does not imply that fulfilment means the negation of what is established and developed in human history. Each moment of histody stands under the possibility of an ultimate fulfilment. The fulfilment is neither a negation of its essential character nor yet a further development of its own inherent capacities. It is rather a completion of its essence by an annihilation of the contradictions which sin has introduced into human life.

(FROM : *Beyond Tragedy*, pp. 3–24.)

4 'WE ARE MEN AND NOT GOD'
(On the theology of Karl Barth)

[This extract illustrates the reaction of a leading exponent of 'Anglo-Saxon' theology to the 'Continental' theology of Karl Barth. While welcoming the emphasis on the finality of Christ and his work, especially for a time of crisis, Niebuhr fears that Barth's theology 'tempts the Christian to share the victory and the glory of the risen Lord without participating in the crucifixion of the self'. It could be a temptation, implies Niebuhr, to what Bonhoeffer called 'cheap grace'. See Vol. 5, pp. 43ff.]

Beyond the traditional differences between confessions at Amsterdam[1] the most marked theological contrast, apparent at the first Assembly of the World Council, was between what was frequently described as the 'Continental theology' and what was with equal inaccuracy known as the 'Anglo-Saxon

[1] The first Assembly of the World Council of Churches was held at Amsterdam in 1948. Barth, Niebuhr and Tillich were present. (Ed.)

approach to theology'. Both designations were inaccurate because many Continentals did not share the first approach, and the second was 'Anglo-Saxon' only in the sense that beyond all denominational distinctions in the Anglo-Saxon world, delegates from that world seemed united in their rejection of the Continental position.

Issues Raised by Barth

This position might best be defined as strongly eschatological. This does not mean that it placed its emphasis primarily upon the hope of the culmination of world history in the second coming of Christ, the final judgement, and the general resurrection. If the position is termed eschatological it must be regarded as a form of 'realized eschatology'. Let Karl Bath's words explain the emphasis, since he was the most persuasive spokesman of the position. The assurance, declared Barth, that 'Jesus Christ has already robbed sin, death, the devil and hell of their power and has already vindicated divine and human justice in his person' ought to persuade us 'even on this first day of our deliberations that the care of the church and the care of the world is not our care. Burdened with this thought we could straighten nothing out.' For the final root of human disorder is precisely 'this dreadful, godless, ridiculous opinion that man is the Atlas who is destined to bear the dome of heaven upon his shoulders'.

No christian would quarrel with the affirmation that the Church finds the true and the new beginning of life and history in the revelatory and redemptive power of our Lord's life, death, and resurrection. The questions which arose at Amsterdam were about the conclusions which were drawn from this article of faith. Did not these conclusions tend to rob the Christian life of its sense of responsibility? Did they not promise a victory for the Christian without a proper emphasis upon repentence? And did they not deal in an irresponsible manner with all the trials and perplexities, the judgements and discriminations, the tasks and duties which Christians face in the daily round of their individual and collective life?

The Testimony of St Paul

The first conclusion which Barth drew from the Christian

certainty that Christ has already gained the victory over sin and death was that 'the care of the Church is not our care'. We must rather commit the Church unto the Lord 'who will bring it to pass'. He has called us to be his witnesses but not to be 'his lawyers, engineers, statisticians, and administrative directors'.

One is a little puzzled about this complete rejection of differentiated functions, since the precise point of St Paul's classical chapter on the church as the body of Christ in 1 Corinthians 12 is that there are not only 'diversities of gifts' but also 'differences of administration' and 'diversities of operation' within the church. And St Paul does have a 'care' about the church, which is very relevant to our present ecumenical task. His care is lest diversities of gifts and differences of administration tempt 'the eye to say to the ear, I have no need of thee'. In other words, he is afraid that special gifts and functions within the church may become the occasion of the isolation of one member from another, rather than the basis for their mutual growth in grace. It is in this way that sin enters the church and divides it. If these divisions are to be overcome, must there not be a contrite recognition of the sinful pride in our special gift or function by which we have become divided?

What is that but 'care' about the church? It is the basis of the 'dying with Christ' without which, according to the Scripture, there can be no new and triumphant life with him. The real weakness of this unvarying emphasis upon what we cannot do and upon what Christ has already done is that it tempts the Christian to share the victory and the glory of the risen Lord without participating in the crucifixion of the self, which is the Scriptural presupposition of a new life, for the individual, the church and the nation.

Decrying the Prophetic Function

We are warned with equal emphasis that the 'care of the world is not our care'. We are to beware lest we seem to present a kind of 'Christian Marshall plan'[1] to the nations. This is a wholesome warning against the pet schemes of

[1] The Marshall plan was a scheme initiated by the United States for assisting European countries devastated by the Second World War. (Ed.)

Christian moralists. But does it not annul the church's prophetic function to the nations? Must not the church be busy
in 'the pulling down of strongholds, casting down imaginations
and every thing that exalteth itself against the knowledge of
God and bringing into captivity every thought to the obedience
of Christ'?

In such a day as this we are particularly confronted with
the fact that nations and empires, proud oligarchies and vainglorious races have been 'wounded' by the divine wrath in the
vicissitudes of history and 'have not received correction'. It is
a sobering fact that judgement so frequently leads to despair
rather than to repentance. It is not within the competence of
the Christian church to change despair into repentance. That
possibility is a mystery of divine grace. But it *does* belong to
the 'care' of the church for the world that it so interpret the
judgements under which nations stand, and so disclose their
divine origin, that there is a possibility of repentance.

If the gospel is made to mean merely the assurance of God's
final triumph over all human rebellion, it may indeed save
men from anxious worries. But does it not also save them
prematurely from their own perplexities? It prevents them
from indulging in the vainglorious belief that they can create
the Kingdom of God by their own virtue. But does it remind
them that they are 'workers together with Him'? Is this not,
in short, a very 'undialectical' gospel in which the 'Yes' of the
divine mercy has completely cancelled out the 'No' of the
divine judgement against all human pride and pretension?

What Help for Christians?

The second question one is forced to raise about this emphasis
is whether it has any guidance or inspiration for Christians in
the day-to-day decisions which are the very woof and warp of
our existence. Barth insists that we have no 'systems of
economic and political principles to offer the world'. We can
present it only 'with a revolutionary hope'. This emphasis has
its limited validity. Christianity is too simply equated by many
with some simple system of 'Christian economics' or 'Christian
sociology'. But Barth's teachings seem to mean that we can,
as Christians, dispense with the principles of justice which,
however faulty, represent the cumulative experience of the race

in dealing with the vexing problems of man's relations to his fellows.

We ought indeed to have a greater degree of freedom from all traditions, even the most hallowed, as we seek to establish and re-establish community in our torn world. But freedom over law cannot mean emancipation from the tortuous and difficult task of achieving a tolerable justice. It is certainly not right for Christians to leave it to the 'pagans' of our day to walk the tightrope of our age, which is strung over the abyss of war and tyranny, seeking by patience and courage to prevent war on the one hand and the spread of tyranny on the other, while the Christians rejoice in a 'revolutionary hope' in which all these anxieties of human existence, and the particular anxieties of our age, are overcome proleptically. It is particularly wrong if we suggest to these pagans that we have no immediate counsel in the present perplexity but that we will furnish a 'sign' of the 'coming Kingdom' by some heroic defiance of malignant power, if the situation becomes desperate enough. We will not counsel any community that this or that course might lead to tyranny. We will merely prepare ourselves to defy tyranny when it is full blown.

'Crisis' Theology Gone to Seed

Here there are suggestions of a 'crisis' theology, but not in the connotation originally intended. It is only fair to Barth and to those for whom he speaks to acknowledge gratefully the great contributions which this theology made to the struggle against tyranny in recent decades. Its interpretation of the Christian faith helped to create a heroic heedlessness, a disposition to follow the Scriptural injunction, 'Be careful in nothing'. This resulted in a very powerful witness to Christ in the hour of crisis. But perhaps this theology is constructed too much for the great crises of history. It seems to have no guidance for a Christian statesman for our day. It can fight the devil if he shows both horns and cloven feet. But it refuses to make discriminating judgements about good and evil if the evil shows only one horn or the half of a cloven foot.

There is a special pathos in the fact that so many of the Christian leaders of Germany are inclined to follow this form of flight from daily responsibilities and decisions, because they are trying to extend the virtue of yesterday to cover the problems of today. Yesterday they discovered that the church may be an ark in which to survive a flood. Today they seem so enamored of this special function of the church that they have decided to turn the ark into a home on Mount Ararat and live in it perpetually.

Barth is as anxious to disavow any special responsibilities in our debate with a secular culture on the edge of despair as in our engagement with a civilization on the edge of disaster. We are not to worry about this 'godless' age. It is no more godless than any other age, just as the evil in our day is neither more nor less than that of any previous period. We seem always to be God rather than men in this theology, viewing the world not from the standpoint of the special perplexities and problems of given periods but *sub specie aeternitatis.*

Have We Nothing to Say ?

In any event, says Barth, we are not to enter into debate with the secularism of our age. With a special dig at his old opponent Brunner, who had analysed the 'axioms' of secularism to prove that they were filled with idolatry, Barth warned that we had nothing special to say to the godless people of our age which we would not have said in any age. What we have to say to them is that 'Jesus Christ died and rose again for them and has become their divine brother and redeemer'.

Does this mean that St Paul had no right to analyse the meaning of the yearning of his day for the 'unknown God' and prove its relevance for the gospel? When Julian Huxley, for instance, writes a book, *Man in the Modern World,* in which he manages to distil every error of modern man about himself and his destiny, his virtue and his wisdom, is the Christian apologist to refrain from every apologetic assault upon some of the absurdities of these modern beliefs? Is he merely to assure Mr Huxley that Christ died for him, even though Mr Huxley could not, in his present state of belief possibly understand why anyone should need to die for us?

One sees that the church is as rigorously prohibited from turning a furrow in the field of culture as in the field of social relations. Let the church remain an ark, ready to receive those who are fleeing the next flood. If, meanwhile, weeds should grow in the garden of either culture or civilization that is not surprising, since the church knows *a priori* that weeds grow in every human garden.

With the fullest appreciation of what this theology did to puncture the illusions of churchmen, theologians, and moralists, one must insist that this is not the whole gospel. It warned the church rightly that it must bear witness, not to its own power but to the power of God, not to its capacity to build the Kingdom but to the Kingdom which has been established by divine grace.

But the Christian faith, which can easily degenerate into a too simple moralism, may also degenerate into a too simple determinism and irresponsibility when the divine grace is regarded as a way of escape from, rather than a source of engagement with, the anxieties, perplexities, sins, and pretensions of human existence. The certainty of the final inadequacy of the 'wisdom of the world' must not be allowed to become the source of cultural obscurantism. The Christian must explore every promise and every limit of the cultural enterprise. The certainty of the final inadequacy of every form of human justice must not lead to defeatism in our approach to the perplexing problems of social justice in our day. The possibilities as well as the limits of every scheme of justice must be explored. The certainty that every form of human virtue is inadequate in the sight of God must not tempt us to hide our talent in the ground.

One of the tasks of an ecumenical movement is to prevent a one-sided statement of the many-sided truth of the gospel. 'Narrow is the way which leadeth unto life.' There is an abyss on each side of that narrow way. Anyone who is too fearful of the abyss on the one side will fall into the abyss on the other side. We 'Anglo-Saxons' who object to this one-sided emphasis may be corrupted by many Pelagian and semi-Pelagian heresies. We stand in need of correction. But we also have the duty to correct.

We are embarrassed about our correction because we cannot deny that this 'Continental' theology outlines the final pinnacle of the Christian faith and hope with fidelity to the Scriptures. Yet it requires correction, because it has obscured the foothills where human life must be lived. It started its theological assault decades ago with the reminder that we are men and not God, and that God is in the heavens and that we are on earth. The wheel is come full circle. It is now in danger of offering a crown without a cross, a triumph without a battle, a scheme of justice without the necessity of discrimination, a faith which has annulled rather than transmuted perplexity—in short, a too simple and premature escape from the trials and perplexities, the duties and tragic choices, which are the condition of our common humanity. The Christian faith knows of a way through these sorrows, but not of a way around them.

(FROM: D. B. Robertson (Ed.), *Essays in Applied Christianity*, by Reinhold Niebuhr, pp. 168–75.)

5 THE CHRISTIAN CHURCH IN A SECULAR AGE

[Like Bultmann and Bonhoeffer, Niebuhr gave a good deal of thought to the problems of communicating the Christian gospel in an intelligible way to a society whose assumptions are basically 'secular'. Strictly speaking, Niebuhr argues, the Western world is still not yet thoroughgoingly 'secular'. There is too much diffused religiosity (often of a pantheistic kind) and 'religious' humanism (a belief that man has some transcendental significance) for that to be the case. In this kind of 'secularism' there is still a sort of religion since an ultimate trust (cf. Tillich's 'Ultimate Concern') is placed in the possibilities of human intelligence and/or virtue. There is also, significantly a moral fervour and passion for justice in much so-called 'humanism' which reminds one of religion. The basic issue at stake, for Niebuhr, is whether we are to conceive human life and destiny in terms of tragedy (noble, impressive, but doomed to meaninglessness) or in terms of redemption (that there is a 'beyond tragedy'). Tillich expresses the same idea as the choice between 'the courage of resignation' (Stoicism) and 'the courage to be'. (See his *The Courage to be*.)

This extract is a good example of Niebuhr's theological appraisal of the modern political, social and cultural scene. In particular it illustrates his suspicion of a theology which so emphasises human sin and impotence (this is what Niebuhr found in Barth) as to engender a neglect of problems of social justice.]

For the past two hundred years the Christian Church has been proclaiming its gospel in a world which no longer accepted the essentials of the Christian Faith. The Western world, particularly the more advanced industrial nations, has come increasingly under the sway of what has been called a secular culture. Secularism is most succinctly defined as the explicit disavowal of the sacred. The holy in every religion is that reality upon which all things depend, in terms of which they are explained and by which they are judged. It is the ultimate mystery, but also the ultimate source of all meaning. For the Christian Faith holiness is ascribed only to the God who is the Creator, Judge and Redeemer of the world. The world is made and sustained by Him. Its historical realities are thus the fruits of His creative will. The world is judged by Him. Its sins stand under His divine judgement. The world is redeemed by Him. Without His grace mediated through Christ, human existence remains a problem to itself, being unable to escape by any effort of its own from the contradictions of a sinful existence.

THE RELIGION OF SECULARISM

In contrast to this faith, modern secularism has been interpreted by the Christian Church too much in terms of secularism's own disavowal of religious faith. Strictly speaking, there is no such thing as secularism. An explicit denial of the sacred always contains some implied affirmation of a holy sphere. Every explanation of the meaning of human existence must avail itself of some principle of explanation which cannot be explained. Every estimate of values involves some criterion of value which cannot be arrived at empirically. Consequently the avowedly secular culture of today turns out upon close examination to be either a pantheistic religion which identifies existence in its totality with holiness, or a rationalistic humanism for which human reason is essentially god or a vitalistic humanism which worships some unique or particular vital force in the individual or the community as its god, that is, as the object of its unconditioned loyalty.

This latter faith, the product of the romantic movement in Western civilization, is the most obvious form of idolatry. It is also the most explicitly religious. Its emergence, particularly on the European Continent, in these latter days of a dying bourgeois culture, proves the irrelevance of critical categories which imply a simple and unqualified contrast between the religious and the secular. There are no irreligious cultures; and if there were, it could not be assumed that a religious culture is intrinsically superior to an irreligious one. The question is not whether we worship a god. That is not the question, on the one hand, because all men do, whether implicitly or explicitly; and on the other hand, the worship of false gods is in no sense preferable to complete agnosticism, if the latter were possible.

The civilization and culture in which we are called upon to preach the Christian gospel is, in other words, not irreligious, but a devotee of a very old religion, dressed in a new form. It is the old religion of self-glorification. This is a very old religion because it involves the quintessence of human sin, as defined by St Paul in the first chapter of Romans. Speaking of the Gentiles and their culpability in the sight of God he declares: 'So that they are without excuse: because that, when they knew God, they glorified Him not as God, neither were thankful; but became vain in their imaginations, and their foolish heart was darkened. Professing themselves to be wise, they became fools [and what an accurate description that is of the vainglory of our modern era], and changed the glory of the uncorruptible God into an image made like to corruptible man, and to birds and four-footed beasts, and creeping things.'

Every form of modern secularism contains an implicit or explicit self-glorification and deification in the sense described in the Letter to the Romans. Humanistic rationalism, forgetting that human reason as well as human physical existence is a derived, dependent, created and finite reality, makes it into a principle of interpretation of the meaning of life; and believes that its gradual extension is the guarantee of the ultimate destruction of evil in history. It mistakes the image of God in man for God Himself. It does not realize that the freedom by

which man is endowed in his rational nature is the occasion for
his sin as well as the ground of morality. It does not understand that by this reason nature's harmless will-to-live is transmuted into a sinful will-to-power. It is by this reason that men
make pretentious claims for their partial and relative insights,
falsely identifying them with absolute truth. Thus rationalism
always involves itself in two descending scales of self-deifica-
tion of humanity in abstract terms ends as the deification of a
particular type of man, who supposedly possesses ultimate
insights. In Aristotelian rationalism this latter development is
expressed in the deification of the aristocrat, whom to glorify
the slave exists. In modern rationalism the final result is a
glorification of bourgeois perspectives.

The recent emergence of a more explicit type of self-glorification in race, State and nation, in religions of Blut und
Boden[1] represents the victory of romanticism over rationalism,
to speak in purely cultural terms. More profoundly considered,
this romantic development is a cynical reaction to the hypo-
critical pretensions of the rationalists. Let those of us who
live in such parts of Western civilization in which the old
rational humanism and universalism is not yet completely
disintegrated guard ourselves against premature self-righteous
judgements. It may be that our type of humanism represents
a more sincere attempt to establish universal values and
expresses an honest devotion to European civilization rather
than to the defiant strength of a particular nation. But on the
other hand, this bourgeois humanism tends to be oblivious to
its own partial, national and bourgeois perspectives. Having
erroneously identified its truth with the eternal truth, it naturally elicits the reaction of a curious kind of cynical romanticism. It is not without significance that rational humanism is
still most robust in the nations which hold a dominant position,
politically and economically, in the Western world, more
particularly the Anglo-Saxon nations; while what we abhor as
primitivistic romanticism flourishes in the less satisfied nations.
Hypocrisy and implicit or covert self-glorification are always
the particular temptation of the victors; and cynicism and a
more explicit self-glorification the sin of the vanquished. The
necessity of compensating for outraged self-esteem is the cause

[1] 'Blood and soil'—a reference to Nazism (Ed.).

of this greater degree of explicitness in the deification of self.

The whole story of modern culture might be truly chronicled in terms of the Parable of the Prodigal Son. The more rational- istic humanism is the son in the first stages of his emancipation from his father. The temper of modern culture is expressed quite precisely in the words of the son: 'Father, give me the portion of goods that falleth to me.' Our civilization did not want to recognize its dependence upon a divine father, who is the source of all life and the judge of all human actions. It wanted an autonomous culture. It separated the 'goods that falleth to me' from the divine patrimony and forgot the dangers of anarchy in this independence. The more romantic type of modern humanism, as revealed in the religio-political movements of the Continent, represent a more advanced state of disintegration. Here the son is 'wasting his substance in riotous living', a civilization allowing the vital energies of peoples and nations to express themselves in anarchic conflict with one another, and insisting that any vital or unique energy is morally self-justifying. The 'mighty famine' when the son begins to be in want is still in the future, but our civilization is destined for such a catastrophe as so certain a consequence of the anarchy of its conflicting national passions and ambitions, that one may well speak of it as part of the contemporary picture.

To leave for a moment the Parable of the Prodigal Son, a further reaction to bourgeois rationalism and humanism must be recorded which seeks to eliminate the errors of this domi- nant form of secularism. I refer to Marxism and the revolt of the proletarians in the Western world against the privileged sections of the community. In this newer form of humanism there is an explicit recognition of the finiteness of the human mind and the relation of human ideals to human interests; to the sinfulness, in short, of all human culture. Yet this very philosophy which sees the pretensions of all 'the wise, the mighty and the noble' so clearly insists that it will be able to arrive at an absolute and universal position. In this creed the life of the proletariat has some mystic union with the absolute.

Here then we have a nice combination of the romantic and the rationalistic strains in modern culture, a glorification of the vitality of the burden bearers of the world as the instrument of an ultimate universalistic humanism; but no recognition that this fateful class is also composed of sinful men and that their sin will become more apparent as soon as they cease to be the oppressed and become the victors. Inasfar as Marxism seeks to establish genuinely universal values it must not be equated with the fascism which defies every common interest in the name of its own self-justifying vitality. Nor can its superiority over the pretentious rationalism of bourgeois life be denied. But unfortunately, as every culture which is not confronted with the one holy God, the Creator, Lord and Judge of the world, it also ends in the sin of self-glorification.

THE MESSAGE OF REPENTANCE

The question is, what shall the Christian Church say to this modern culture, which began its adventure in autonomy with such gay self-assurance, which is already so deeply involved in 'riotous living' and which faces so certain a doom of a mighty famine?

We must, of course, preach the gospel to this, as to every generation. Our gospel is one which assures salvation in the Cross of Christ to those who heartily repent of their sins. It is a gospel of the Cross; and the Cross is a revelation of the love of God only to those who have first stood under it as a judgement. It is in the Cross that the exceeding sinfulness of human sin is revealed. It is in the Cross that we become conscious how, not only what is worst, but what is best in human culture and civilization is involved in man's rebellion against God. It was Roman law, the pride of all pagan civilization, and Hebraic religion, the acme of religious devotion, which crucified the Lord. Thus does the Cross reveal the problem of all human culture and the dilemma of every human civilization.

Repentance is the first key into the door of the Kingdom of God. God resisteth the proud and giveth grace to the humble. Whenever men trust their own righteousness, their own achievements, whenever they interpret the meaning of life in terms of the truth in their own culture or find in their own capacities a sufficient steppingstone to the Holy and the

Divine, they rest their life upon a frail reed which inevitably breaks and leaves their life meaningless.

Perhaps that is why the truest interpretations of the Christian faith have come in moments of history when civilizations were crumbling and the processes of history and the judgements of God had humbled human arrogance. The faith of the Hebrew prophets was thus formulated when the culture religion of Israel was threatened and finally overcome by the mighty civilizations of Assyria and Babylon. Augustine wrote the *City of God* when Roman civilization, once mighty enough to seem identical with civilization itself, had become the helpless victim of barbarians; and the renewal of the Christian gospel in the Protestant Reformation was, historically speaking, the consequence as well as the cause of the crumbling of a once proud medieval civilization. Proud men and successful civilizations find it difficult to know God, because they are particularly tempted to make themselves God. That is why 'not many mighty, not many noble, not many wise after the flesh are called'. Without the godly sorrow that worketh repentance there can be no salvation.

We must of course preach the gospel to their as to every generation. Our gospel is one which assures salvation in the love of Christ to men who repent of their sins. The love at the heart of the Cross; and the Cross is a revelation of the love

THE MESSAGE OF HOPE

Just as the Christian gospel calls the proud to repent, it assures those who despair of a new hope. It is interesting how every religion which imparts a superficial meaning to life, and grounds that meaning in a dubious sanctity, finally issues in despair. Those who make the family their god must despair when the family is proved to be only a little less mortal than the individual. Those who make a god of their nation must despair when the might of their nation crumbles, as every creaturely and sinful might must: 'For we are consumed by thine anger and by thy wrath are we troubled.' That is the despair which awaits many a young nationalistic pagan of Europe today. They might even, if they could see truly, despair in the triumph of their nation, for the nation in triumph is less worthy of reverence than the nation in defeat. Pride accentuates its sins, and there are no sufferings to prompt pity as a handmaiden of love in the heart of the patriot.

Every humanistic creed is a cosmos of meaning sustained by a thin ice on the abysmal deeps of meaninglessness and chaos. Only the faith in God, who has been 'our dwelling place in all generations', and who was God 'before the mountains were brought forth or ever the earth and the world were made', can survive the vicissitudes of history, can rescue human existence from the despair in which it is periodically involved by its sinful pretensions, and the tragic disappointment of its facile hopes.

The fulfilment of life, according to our Christian faith, is possible only through the mercy of God. All superficial questions about the meaning of life, all simple religions which imagine that faith in any god is better than no faith at all, fail to recognize that the ultimate question is not whether life has a meaning (which it must have or no one could live), but whether or not the meaning is tragic. The only serious competitor to Christianity as a spiritual religion is Buddhism, and in Buddhism life is conceived in terms of pure tragedy. Christianity is a faith which takes us through tragedy to beyond tragedy, by way of the Cross to a victory in the Cross. The God whom we worship takes the contradictions of human existence into Himself. This knowledge is a stumbling block to the Jews, and to the Gentiles foolishness, but to them that are called it is the power and the wisdom of God. This is a wisdom beyond human knowledge, but not contrary to human experience. Once known, the truth of the gospel explains our experiences which remain inexplicable on any other level. Through it we are unable to understand life in all of its beauty and its terror, without being beguiled by its beauty or driven to despair by its terror.

NOT OF THE WORLD, BUT IN THE WORLD

While the gospel which we preach reveals a world which in its ground and its fulfilment transcends human history, it does not abstract us from this present history with all of its conflicts and tragic disappointments of arrogant hopes. We are in the world, and God's Will, His Judgement and His Mercy impinge upon our daily actions and historic problems. We must bring forth fruits meet for repentance. What can those fruits be but the fruits of 'love, joy, peace?' when the Church proclaims the love commandment to the world as the law of God it must guard against the superficial moralism of telling the world that it can save itself if men will only stop being selfish and learn to be loving. We dare not forget that in us, as well as in those who do not acknowledge the Christian gospel, there is a law in our members that wars against the law that is in our mind. The law of love is not kept simply by being preached. Yet it is the law of life and must be both preached and practised. It is a terrible heresy to suggest that, because the world is sinful, we have a right to construct a Machiavellian politics or a Darwinian sociology as normative for Christians.

What is significant about the Christian ethic is precisely this: that it does not regard the historic as normative. Man may be, as Thomas Hobbes[1] observed, a wolf to his fellowman. But this is not his essential nature. Let Christianity beware, particularly radical Protestanism, that it does not accept the habits of a sinful world as the norms of a Christian collective life. For the Christian only the law of love is normative. He would do well to remember that he is a sinner who has never perfectly kept the law of God. But neither must he forget that he is a child of God who stands under that law. Much of what passes for theological profundity today is no more than a subtle re-enactment of the part of the son in the Lord's Parable who promised to do the father's will and did not, leaving his will to be done by the son who had refused to promise it. How accurately that little parable of Christ pictures the superior passion for human justice of many outside the Church as against those who are in it. Frequently, believing Christians are tempted by their recognition of the sinfulness of human existence to disavow their own responsibility for a tolerable justice in the world's affairs. Justice is not love. Justice presupposes the conflict of life with life and seeks to mitigate it. Every relative justice therefore stands under the judgement of the law of love, but it is also an approximation of it.

A Christian pessimism which becomes a temptation to irresponsibility toward all those social tasks which constantly

[1] Thomas Hobbes (1588–1679), English philosopher. (Ed.)

confront the life of men and nations, tasks of ordering the productive labour of men, of adjudicating their conflicts, of arbitrating their divergent desires, of raising the level of their social imagination and increasing the range of their social sympathies, such a pessimism cannot speak redemptively to a world constantly threatened by anarchy and suffering from injustice. The Christian gospel which transcends all particular and contemporary social situations can be preached with power only by a Church which bears its share of the burdens of immediate situations in which men are involved, burdens of establishing peace, of achieving justice, and of perfecting justice in the spirit of love. Thus is the Kingdom of God which is not of this world made relevant to every problem of the world.

THE DANGER OF PROFANIZATION

If the problem of presenting the Christian ethic to a non-Christian world without the spirit of self-righteousness is difficult, an even more far-reaching problem is the presentation of the gospel to a secular age. The truths of the Christian gospel are simple and clear. But it is not easy for any human institution to mediate them without pride or hypocrisy; and the Church is a human institution, though it is that institution where it is known that all human life stands under a divine judgement and within a divine mercy. The real difficulty of preaching the gospel of God's mercy to the prodigal son, our modern culture, lies in the temptation to play the part of the elder brother in the Lord's Parable. One might indeed elaborate this Parable without disloyalty to its meaning, with the suggestion that the younger son might well have been prompted to leave his father's house because of the insufferable self-righteousness of the elder brother. At any rate, it is quite obvious that no Christian Church has a right to preach to a so-called secular age without a contrite recognition of the shortcomings of historic Christianity which tempted the modern age to disavow its Christian faith.

Secularism is, on the one hand, the expression of man's sinful self-sufficiency. It may be, on the other hand, a reaction to profanity. Some men are atheists because of a higher implicit theism than that professed by believers. They reject God because His name has been taken in vain, and they are unable to distinguish between His Holiness and its profanization. It is popular today in Christian circles to speak somewhat contemptuously of the errors and illusions of the secular culture which challenged Christianity so optimistically in the last two centuries and finds itself in such confusion today. It would be well to remember, however, that the primary conscious motive of this secularism (whatever may have been its unconscious and more sinful motives) was to break the chains which a profane Christianity had placed upon man.

A profane Christianity, like the elder brother, ostensibly maintains its sense of dependence upon the Father, but it uses this relationship to satisfy a sinful egotism. It falsely identifies its relative and partial human insights with God's wisdom, and its partial and relative human achievements with God's justice. A profane Christianity falsely identifies the Church with the Kingdom of God. Since the historic Church is always touched with human finiteness, is subject to sociological forces and pressures, and victim of the prejudices and illusions of particular ages, any tendency to obscure or deny this fact becomes the final and most terrible expression of human sinfulness. Of that sin no Church has been free.

Protestants may believe, and not without a measure of truth, that this sin of profaning the Holiness of God, of using His Name in vain, is a particular danger in Catholicism, for Catholicism has a doctrine of the Church in which what is human and what is divine in the Church is constantly subject to a confused identification of the one with the other. Yet no historic Christian institution is free of this sin. Every vehicle of God's grace, the preacher of the word, the prince of the Church, the teacher of theology, the historic institution, the written word, the sacred canon, all these are in danger of being revered as if they were themselves divine. The aura of the divine word, which is transmitted through them, falsely covers their human frailties. The Christian Church has never followed St Paul rigorously enough in his disavowal of divinity: 'And when the people saw what Paul had done they lifted up their voices saying, in the speech of Lyconia: The Gods have come down to us in the likeness of men . . . which when the Apostles

Paul and Barnabas heard of they rent their clothes and ran in among the people crying out and saying, Sirs, why do ye these things? We also are men of like passions with you and preach unto you, that ye should turn from these vanities unto the living God, which made heaven and earth and the sea and all things that are therein' (Acts 14:11–15).

SECULARISM AS A REACTION AGAINST A PROFANE CHRISTIANITY

Modern secularism was forced to resist a profanization of the holiness of God both in the realm of the truth and in the realm of the good, in both culture and ethics. In the realm of culture the Christian religion was tempted to complete the incompleteness of all human culture by authoritative dicta, supposedly drawn from Scripture. It forgot that theology is a human discipline subject to the same relativities as any other human discipline. If modern culture was wrong in regarding the Anselmic axiom *'Credo ut intelligam'*[1] as absurd because it failed to understand that reason cannot function without the presuppositions of faith, Christian culture was wrong in insinuating the specific insights and prejudices of a particular age into the *'credo'*. While modern science was wrong in assuming that its descriptions of detailed historical sequences in nature and history offered an adequate insight into the meaning of life as adequate explanations of detailed sequences and efficient causation.

Thus we have been subjected for centuries to a conflict between a theology which had become a bad science, and a science which implied an unconscious theology, a theology of unconscious presuppositions about the ultimate meaning of life. These presuppositions were doubly wrong. They were wrong in content and erroneous in being implicit rather than explicit. But surely the responsibility for this confusing conflict rests as much with a theology which had become a bad science as with a science which is a bad theology. In one sense all Orthodox Christian theology has been guilty of the sin of profanity. It has insisted on the literal and historic truth of

[1] 'I believe in order to understand' (Ed.).

its myths, forgetting that it is the function and character of religious myth to speak of the eternal in relation to time, and that it cannot therefore be a statement of temporal sequences.

No Christian theology, worthy of its name, can therefore be without gratitude to the forces of modern secularism inasfar as their passion for truth was a passion for God. They failed indeed to recognize that every search for truth begins with a presupposition of faith. They did not know for this reason how vulnerable they were to the sneer of Pilate: 'What is truth?'; and they could not consequently appreciate the affirmation of Christ: 'I am the truth.' But this secularization of truth is no more culpable than the religious profanization of truth which blandly appropriates the truth in Christ for every human vagary and prejudice, for every relative insight and temporal perspective.

The profanity of historic Christianity in regard to the problem of righteousness has been even more grievous than in regard to the problem of truth. Every human civilization is a compromise between the necessities and contigencies of nature and the Kingdom of God with its absolute love commandment. This is as true of a Christian as of an unchristian civilization. In a Christian, as well as in an unchristian civilization, the strong are tempted to exploit the weak, the community is tempted to regard itself as an end in itself, and the rulers are tempted to use their power for their own advantage. When the welter of relative justice and injustice, which emerges out of this conflict and confluence of forces, is falsely covered with the aura of the divine, and when the preservation of such a civilization is falsely enjoined as a holy duty, and when its rebels and enemies are falsely regarded as enemies of God, it is only natural that those who are most conscious of the injustices of a given social order, because they suffer from them, should adopt an attitude of cynical secularism toward the pretensions of sanctity made in behalf of a civilization. A profanization of the holiness of God leads inevitably to an effort to eliminate the sacred from human life. Invariably this effort is partially informed by a covert and implicit sense of the sacred, morally higher than the historical sanctity against which it protests. One need only study the perverted religious intensity of the nineteenth-century Russian nihilists to understand how a warfare against God may be prompted by a prophetic passion for God and scorn for the dubious political divinities which seek to borrow His holiness.

It is impossible to understand the secularism of either the commercial classes or the radical proletarians of the past hundred and fifty years if it is not appreciated to what degree this secularism represents a reaction to the too intimate and organic relation of Christianity with a feudal society. The priest of religion and the landlord of an agrarian society were too closely related to each other and the former was too frequently the apologist and auxiliary gendarme of the latter.

It may seem that this charge falls more heavily upon Catholicism than upon Protestantism, not only because of the historic relation of the former with a medieval culture and feudal civilization, but also because the latter is less prone to identify itself with the detailed economic and political arrangements of any society. But with its higher degree of detachment Protestantism has sometimes also revealed a higher degree of social irresponsibility. It has allowed its pessimism to betray it into a negative sanctification of a given social order on the assumption that any given order is preferable to anarchy and that the disturbance of the *status quo* might lead to anarchy.

Thus Catholicism and Protestantism, between them, have exhausted the possibilities of error in Christianity's relation to society. In either case peace and order through power were estimated too highly and the inevitable injustice of every stabilization of power was judged too leniently. Frequently Christianity was content to regard deeds of personal generosity and charity as adequate expressions of the Christian love commandment within a civilization in which every basic relationship was a complete denial of that commandment.

The secularism both of our modern bourgeois civilization and of the more proletarian civilizations which threaten to replace it, is therefore something more than the religion of self-glorification. It combines this sin with a passion for justice which frequently puts the historic Church to shame. If the Christian Church is to preach its gospel effectively to men of such a culture, it must understand the baffling mixture of a new profanity and resistance to an old profanity which is comprehended in this culture.

JUDGEMENT MUST BEGIN AT THE HOUSE OF GOD

Such a recognition is the clue to the problem of an effective proclamation of the Christian gospel in our day. If we preach repentance, it must be repentance for those who accept the Lord as well as for those who pretend to deny Him. If we preach the judgement of God upon a sinful world, it must be judgement upon us as well as upon those who do not acknowledge His judgements. If we preach the mercy of God, it must be with a humble recognition that we are in need of it as much as those who do not know God's mercy in Christ. If we preach the obligation of the love commandment, the preacher must know that he violates that commandment as well as those who do not consciously accept its obligation. Nothing is cheaper and more futile than the preaching of a simple moralism which is based upon the assumption that the world need only to be told that selfishness is sin and that love is the law of life to beguile it from the anarchy of sin in which it is at present engulfed. Such a moralism, to which the modern Church is particularly prone, is blind to the real tragedy and persistence of sin in the world.

To preach to others and become ourselves castaways is a peril in which all holy business is done. It is a peril to which the Church must succumb if it does not constantly hear the challenge of God to Jeremiah to 'separate the precious from the vile'; to distinguish between what is genuinely the Lord's will and our will, His holiness and our sin in the work of the Christian Church. The Kingdom of God was ushered in by the preaching of John the Baptist. The most profound element in John's message of repentance was expressed in the words, 'And think not to say within yourselves, We have Abraham to our Father; for I say unto you that God is able of these stones to raise up children unto Abraham.'[1] Not only the racial inheritors of a divine promise are tempted to rest complacently in the assurance 'We have Abraham to our Father.' That is a temptation which assails all inheritors of a divine promise, including the Christian Church, the 'Israel of God.' It is wholesome therefore for the Church to stand under the stinging

[1] Matthew 3:9.

rebuke 'God is able of these stones to raise up children unto Abraham,' a rebuke in the form of a statement of fact which history has validated again and again.

If the conscience of the Church feels the relevance to its own life of that rebuke, it can preach the gospel of a holy God, holy in righteousness and in mercy, without making sinful claims for itself in the name of that holiness, and it will be able to speak to the conscience of this generation, rebuking its sins without assuming a role of self-righteousness and overcoming its despair without finding satisfaction in the sad disillusionment into which the high hopes of modernity have issued.

(FROM: *Christianity and Power Politics*, pp. 203–26.)

FOR FURTHER STUDY AND DISCUSSION

1 How would you define 'humanism'? What are the distinguishing features of what Niebuhr calls 'classical humanism'? How do you account for its continuing appeal. (See Albert Camus, *The Myth of Sisyphus* and *The Rebel*.)

2 Is 'tragedy' incompatible with Christian belief? (See Niebuhr's essay 'Christianity and tragedy' in *Beyond Tragedy*.)

3 What meanings do you attach to 'sin', 'original sin', 'the fall of man'?

4 Construct an imaginary discussion between Bultmann, Tillich, Barth and Niebuhr on the subject of 'Myth'.

5 How do you imagine a conversation between Barth, Bonhoeffer and Niebuhr on 'the Church being in the world but not of it' would have gone?

FOR FURTHER READING

PRINCIPAL WORKS OF REINHOLD NIEBUHR

Moral Man and Immoral Society: a study in ethics and politics, London, 1932.

An interpretation of Christian ethics, London, 1935.

Beyond Tragedy: essays on the Christian interpretation of history, London, 1937.

Christianity and Power Politics, NewYork, Scribner's, 1940.

The Nature and Destiny of Man. Vols. I and II, London, 1941.

The Children of Light and the Children of Darkness: a vindication of democracy and a critique of its traditional defence, London, 1944.

Discerning the signs of the times: sermons for today and tomorrow, London, 1946.

Faith and history: a comparison of Christian and modern views of history, London, 1949.

The Irony of American History, London, 1952.

Christian realism and political problems, London, 1953.

The Self and the Dramas of History, London, 1955.

The Godly and the Ungodly: essays on the religious and secular dimensions of modern life, London, 1958.

SOME BOOKS ON REINHOLD NIEBUHR

Gordon Harland, *The Thought of Reinhold Niebuhr*, New York, 1960.

June Bingham, *Courage to Change*: an introduction to the life and thought of Reinhold Niebuhr, New York, 1961 (very useful for the way it relates the development of Niebuhr's thought to his biography).

FOR GENERAL BACKGROUND READING

John Macquarrie, *Twentieth-century Religious Thought*, 1963.
——, *God-talk*, 1967.
——, *God and Secularity*, 1968.
Frederick Ferré, *Language, Logic and God*, 1962.
——, *Basic Modern Philosophy of Religion*, 1968.
David E. Jenkins, *Guide to the Debate about God*, 1966.
Colin Williams, *Faith in a Secular Age*, 1966.
E. L. Mascall, *The Secularisation of Christianity*, 1965.
H. Gollwitzer, *The Existence of God as confessed by faith*, 1964.
A. M. Ramsey, *God, Christ and the World*, 1969.
T. W. Ogletree, *The Death of God Controversy*, 1966.